バットマン

BATMAN
THE JIRO KUWATA
BATMANGA
VOLUME 2

Written & Illustrated by **JIRO KUWATA**
New Translation by **SHELDON DRZKA**
Lettered by **WES ABBOTT**
BATMAN created by **BOB KANE**

TABLE OF CONTENTS

THE REVENGE OF CLAYFACE 3
THE HANGMAN OF TERROR 69
FIEND OF THE MASQUERADE FESTIVAL 133
MYSTERY OF THE OUTSIDER 193
THE MONSTER OF GORE BAY 258

バットマン
WHETHER IN AMERICA OR JAPAN...
...HE'S TV'S MOST POPULAR STAR, BATMAN!!
★THE REVENGE OF CLAYFACE★
Jiro Kuwata
BATMAN
EXCLUSIVE
JAPANESE VERSION
SHONEN GAHOSHA
© N.P.P. 1966

WE BRING YOU A SPECIAL BULLETIN.

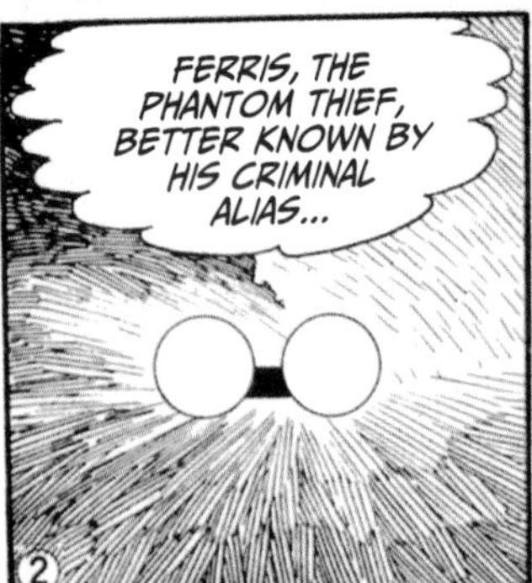
FERRIS, THE PHANTOM THIEF, BETTER KNOWN BY HIS CRIMINAL ALIAS...

...CLAYFACE, HAS BROKEN OUT OF PRISON YET AGAIN!

WE UNDERSTAND THAT FERRIS DOES NOT CURRENTLY HAVE THOSE STRANGE CLAYFACE POWERS...
SFX: WHOOSH

...BUT EVERYONE IN GOTHAM CITY SHOULD STILL TAKE PRECAUTIONS.

WELL, WE KNOW WHERE FERRIS MUST BE HEADING FIRST...

THE CAVE WITH THE POND OF WEIRD GOO!

EXACTLY! IF HE IMMERSES HIMSELF IN THAT LIQUID, HE'LL BECOME CLAYFACE AGAIN!

THIS IS IT.

AFTER WE CAPTURED FERRIS, THE CAVE WAS BLOWN UP.
THERE ISN'T ANYTHING LEFT OF IT.

BUT FERRIS DOESN'T KNOW THAT, SO I'M SURE HE'S ON HIS WAY.

LITTLE KNOWING THAT THERE'S NOT EVEN ONE DROP LEFT OF THAT GUNK!

WELL, THAT'S NOT ENTIRELY TRUE. PROFESSOR ZONE HAS ONE FLASK'S WORTH.

PROFESSOR ZONE? THE ASTRONOMER AND CHEMIST?

PROFESSOR ZONE HEARD ABOUT CLAYFACE AND SCRAMBLED OVER HERE ON THE DAY THE CAVE WAS DUE TO BE DESTROYED.

ACCORDING TO PROFESSOR ZONE...

...ONE NIGHT, A LARGE METEOR FLEW OVER THIS CAVE.

HE RUSHED OVER AS SOON AS HE COULD, BUT THERE WAS NO SIGN OF THE FALLEN METEOR.

HOWEVER, A LIQUID WAS DRIPPING FROM THE CEILING INSIDE THE CAVE, FORMING A PUDDLE BELOW.

SFX: DRIP DRIP DRIP

AT THE TIME, HE THOUGHT IT WAS JUST AN ORDINARY PUDDLE AND WENT HOME...

...BUT WHEN HE HEARD ABOUT CLAYFACE, HE REALIZED THERE WAS PROBABLY A CONNECTION BETWEEN THE PUDDLE AND THAT METEOR.

IN OTHER WORDS, THE METEOR CRASHED INTO THE TOP OF THE CAVE AND ITS LIQUEFIED REMAINS SOAKED INTO THE ROCK, FORMING A PUDDLE INSIDE.

THEN THAT LIQUID IS FROM SPACE?
WE DON'T KNOW FOR SURE YET.

BUT PROFESSOR ZONE SAID HE WANTED TO IDENTIFY IT, SO HE SCOOPED UP A FLASKFUL.

AND WHAT DID HE FIND?

I HAVEN'T HEARD FROM HIM SINCE THEN. I SUPPOSE HE'S STILL WORKING ON IT.

ANYWAY, WE CAN PAY PROFESSOR ZONE A VISIT IN THE MORNING.

SFX: ZOOM

=CHUCKLE= PROFESSOR ZONE, *EH?*

PROFESSOR ZONE'S RESEARCH FACILITY...

SFX: BLUP BLUP BLUP

HMMM...
IT'S ALIVE. THIS LIQUID IS CERTAINLY ALIVE.

THIS IS A LIFE FORM FROM A PLANET OTHER THAN EARTH.

AND IF IT PERMEATES A HUMAN BODY, IT PRODUCES A CHANGE IN THE LIVING CELLS FOR UP TO DAYS.

DURING THAT TIME, IF YOU CONCENTRATE, YOU CAN CHANGE YOUR BODY AT WILL.

WHAT AN AMAZING FORM OF LIFE...

EH?
THAT'S EXACTLY WHAT I WANT.

≈CHUCKLE≈ SOUNDS LIKE YOU DON'T LISTEN TO THE NEWS, PROFESSOR ZONE.
WHAT DO YOU WANT?! WHO ARE YOU?!

SFX: CLIK

FERRIS, THE ESCAPED FELON KNOWN AS CLAYFACE, IS STILL AT LARGE...

Y-YOU'RE...

THAT'S RIGHT! FERRIS, OR CLAYFACE IF YOU LIKE!

BUT I NEED THAT INCREDIBLE JUICE TO GET BACK TO BEING CLAYFACE.

YOU'VE COME HERE FOR THE EXTRATERRESTRIAL LIQUID LIFE?!

NOW YOU GOT THE PICTURE.
THANKS TO THAT IDIOT BATMAN, THE JUICE IN THE CAVE WAS DESTROYED WHEN HE HAD THE PLACE DYNAMITED.

SO YOU GOT THE LAST OF IT RIGHT THERE.

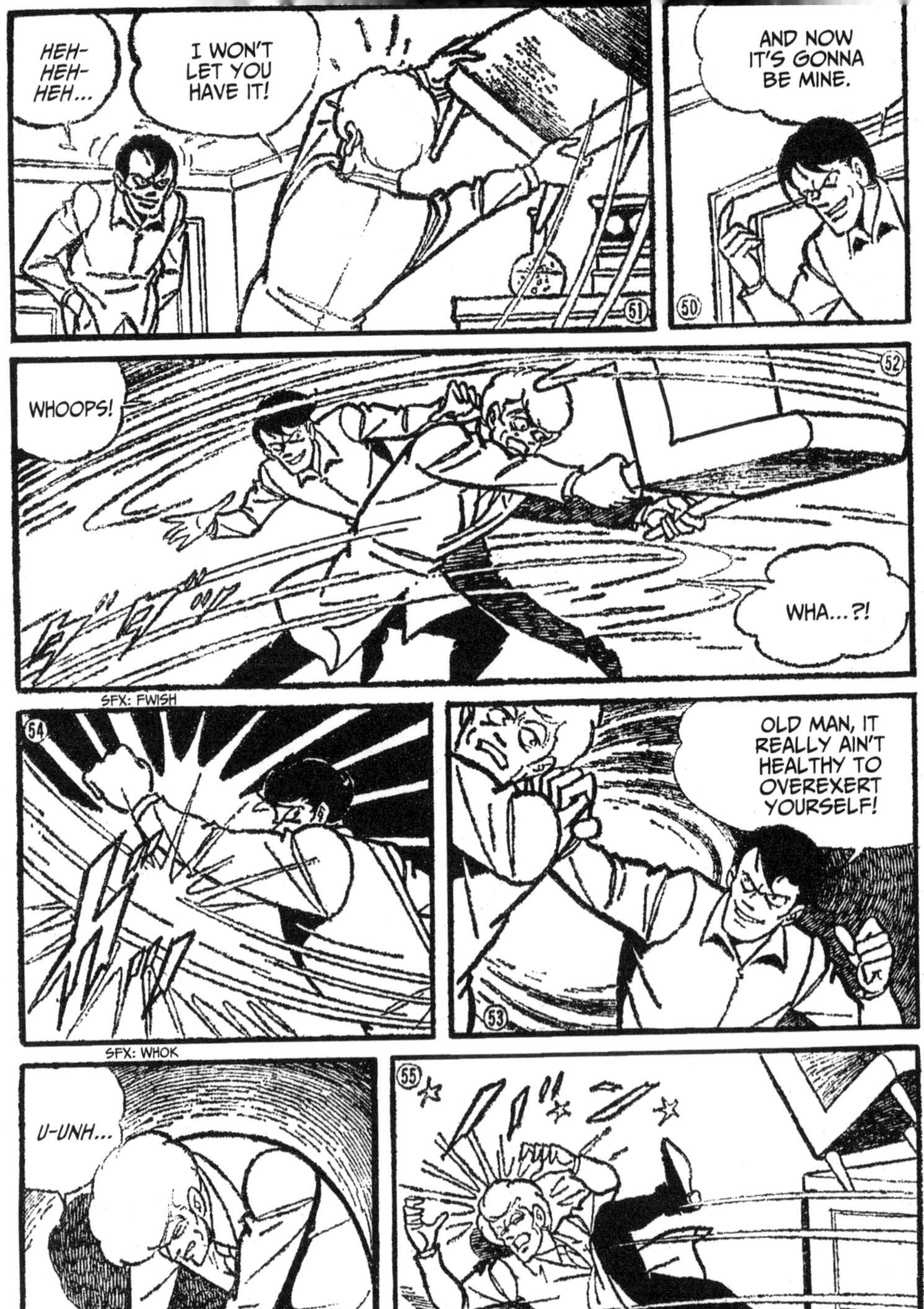
AND NOW IT'S GONNA BE MINE.
I WON'T LET YOU HAVE IT!
HEH-HEH-HEH...
WHOOPS!
WHA...?!
SFX: FWISH
OLD MAN, IT REALLY AIN'T HEALTHY TO OVEREXERT YOURSELF!
SFX: WHOK
SFX: BAM
U-UNH...

≋CHUCKLE≋ NOW I'LL BE ABLE TO BECOME CLAYFACE AGAIN!
THEN I'VE GOT NOTHIN' TO FEAR!

≋CHUCKLE≋ HOW DO YOU PROPOSE TO IMMERSE YOUR BODY IN THAT LITTLE BIT OF LIFE?

WHAT?

THERE ISN'T ENOUGH FOR YOU TO BATHE IN!

HMMM...

WAIT... YOU WERE MUTTERING TO YOURSELF BEFORE I CAME IN.

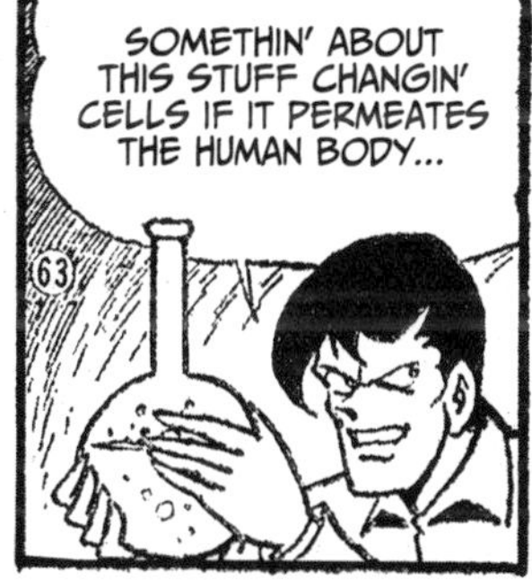
SOMETHIN' ABOUT THIS STUFF CHANGIN' CELLS IF IT PERMEATES THE HUMAN BODY...

IF THAT'S THE CASE, THEN WHO NEEDS A BATH? ALL I GOTTA DO IS DRINK IT UP.

I DON'T KNOW! A DRINKING EXPERIMENT HAS NEVER BEEN DONE WITH IT!

ALL RIGHT, THEN! WE'LL EXPERIMENT ON YOUR BODY!
W-WHAT?!

DRINK IT! THEN WE'LL KNOW WHETHER IT WORKS OR NOT!

N-NO! I WON'T BE A GUINEA PIG!

OH, MY. THIS BOY CERTAINLY HAS A MOUTH ON HIM.

SFX: KRAK

DOWN THE HATCH!

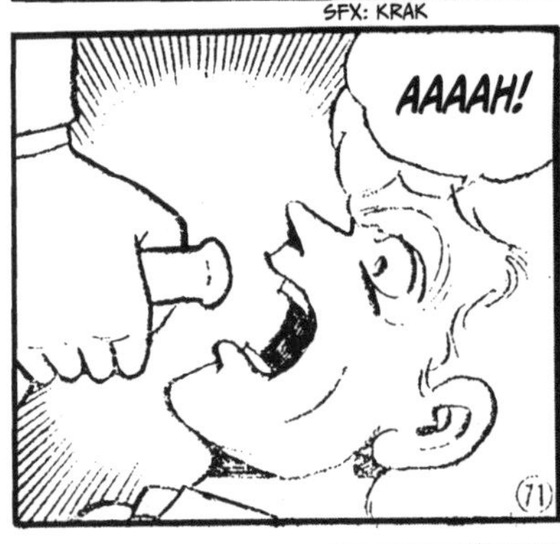
AAAAH!

SFX: FWUMP

WELL? ANYTHING?
COME ON, SAY SOMETHIN'!

OH!

SFX: BLOOP BLOOP

I-IT'S CHANGIN'! PROFESSOR ZONE'S BODY IS TURNIN' INTO CLAY!

JUST LIKE I THOUGHT! THIS STUFF WORKS JUST AS GOOD IF YOU DRINK IT!
WAHAHAHAHAHA!

むく
むく

SFX: BLOOP BLOOP

HUH?

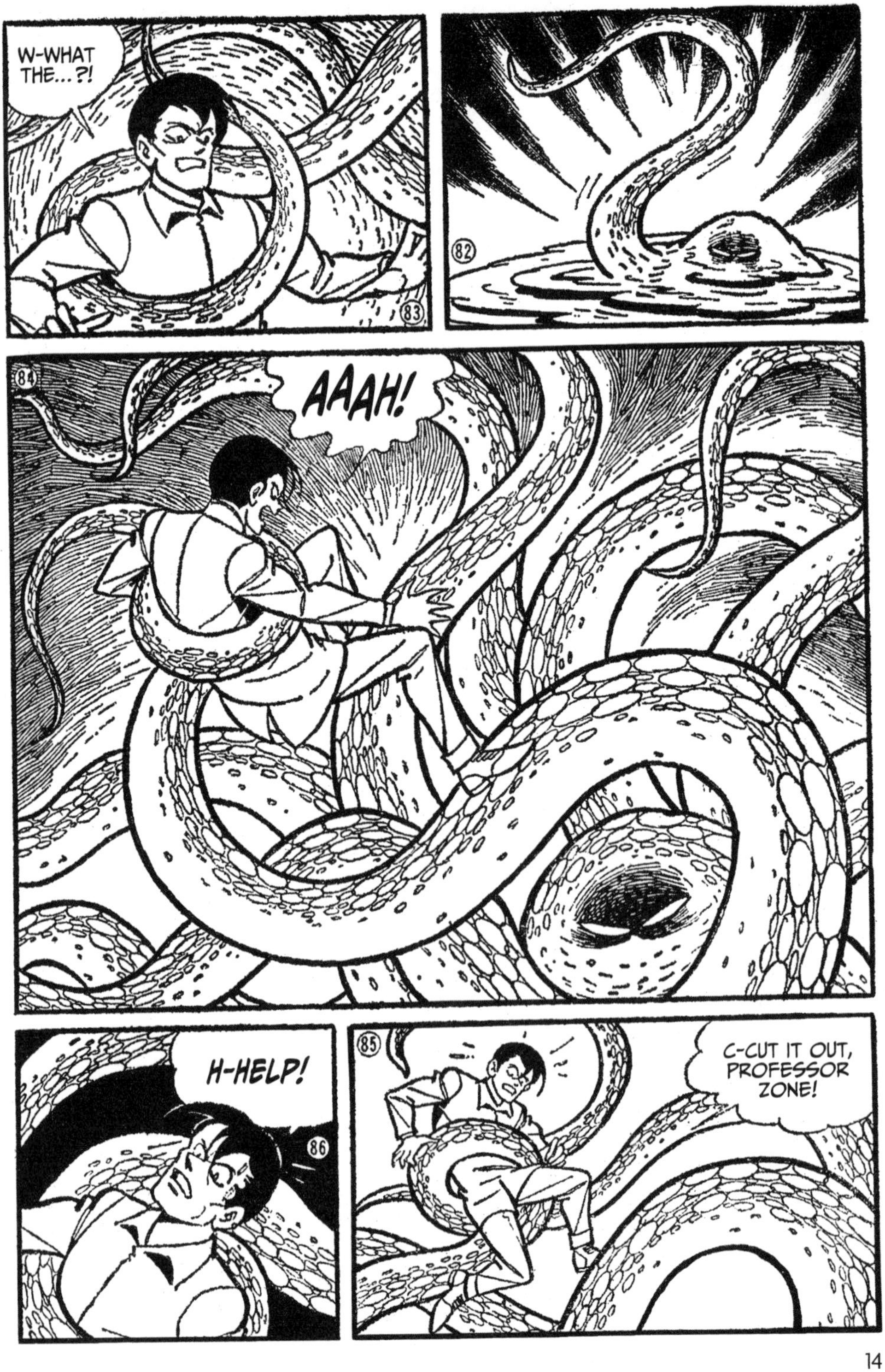

W-WHAT THE...?!

AAAH!

C-CUT IT OUT, PROFESSOR ZONE!

H-HELP!

MEANWHILE, BATMAN AND ROBIN WERE RACING TOWARDS PROFESSOR ZONE'S RESEARCH FACILITY.
SFX: WHOOSH

SFX: WHIZZZ

HEY, BATMAN! WHAT'S THAT?

AH!

SFX: FOOSH

OH, NO! PROFESSOR ZONE'S RESEARCH FACILITY IS BURNING DOWN!

BUT WHAT HAPPENED TO THE PROFESSOR?

PROFESSOR ZONE'S RESEARCH FACILITY HAS BURNT TO THE GROUND.
THE CHARRED, UNIDENTIFIED CORPSE OF ONE MAN WAS DISCOVERED IN THE RUINS, BUT IT'S SPECULATED TO BE PROFESSOR ZONE HIMSELF.

SFX: KLIK

SO PROFESSOR ZONE PERISHED IN THE FIRE...

THEN THAT MYSTERIOUS LIQUID MUST ALSO HAVE BEEN SWALLOWED UP IN FLAMES.

SO NOW WE'LL NEVER KNOW WHAT THAT STUFF WAS.

AND FERRIS IS STILL ON THE LOOSE...

BUT AT LEAST THERE'S NO CHANCE WE'LL EVER SEE CLAYFACE AGAIN, RIGHT?
TRUE...

BUT BATMAN AND ROBIN DON'T KNOW WHAT HAPPENED AT PROFESSOR ZONE'S RESEARCH FACILITY...

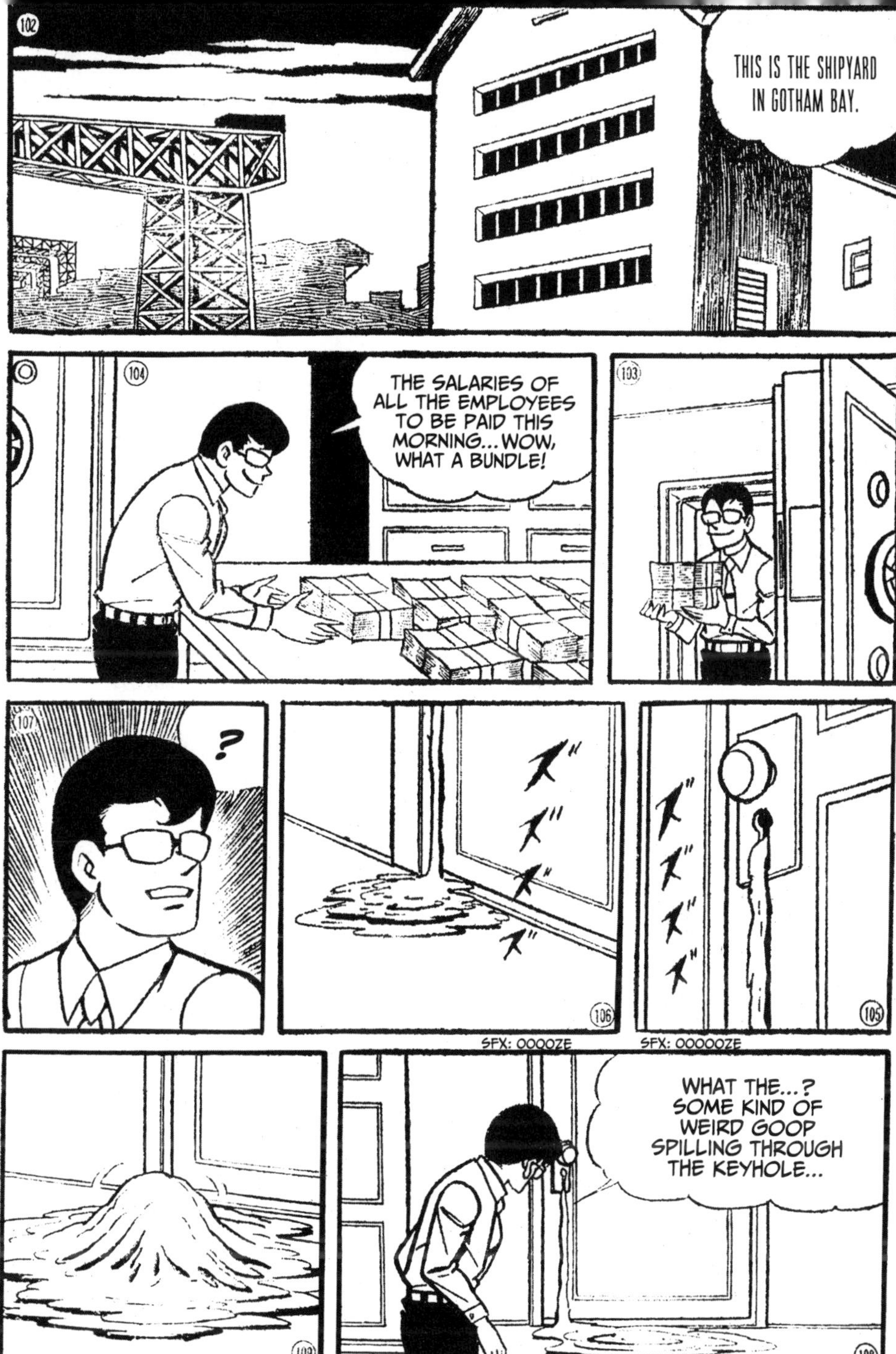
THIS IS THE SHIPYARD IN GOTHAM BAY.
THE SALARIES OF ALL THE EMPLOYEES TO BE PAID THIS MORNING...WOW, WHAT A BUNDLE!
SFX: OOOOZE
SFX: OOOOZE
?
WHAT THE...? SOME KIND OF WEIRD GOOP SPILLING THROUGH THE KEYHOLE...

AAAHHH!

CHUCKLE

CLAYFACE!

T-THE ALARM!

にゅっ

SFX: FWISH

AAAH!

AAARGH!

AAAARRGH!

MEANWHILE, THE BATMOBILE COINCIDENTALLY HAPPENED TO BE ON PATROL IN THAT VERY AREA.

BATMAN! THAT SCREAM!
IT CAME FROM THE OFFICE!

LET'S CHECK IT OUT, ROBIN!

SFX: CRASH

WHAT IS THAT?!

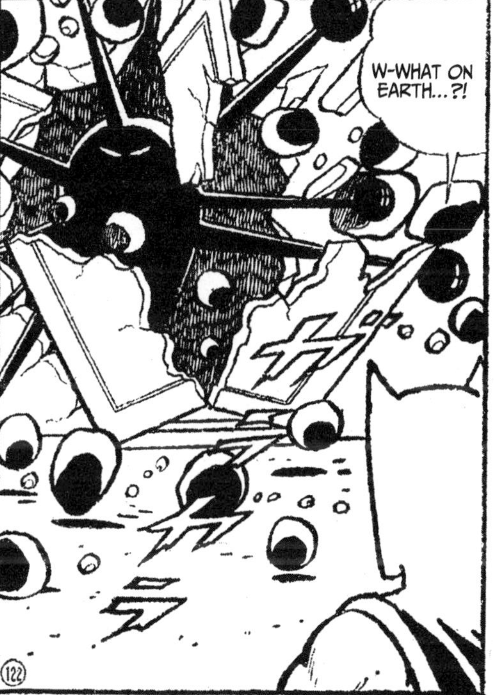
W-WHAT ON EARTH...?!

SFX: CRASH

バットマン
★THE REVENGE OF CLAYFACE Part 2★
BATMAN
EXCLUSIVE
JAPANESE VERSION
SHONEN GAHOSHA
© N.P.P. 1966
Jiro Kuwata

PREVIOUSLY: The mysterious liquid in Professor Zone's possession was Bioplasm, an extraterrestrial life-form. Once inside the human body, it causes cellular transformations, making one able to change shape, becoming a clay-man. Escaped convict Ferris went to Professor Zone's lab to obtain the Bioplasm. By the time Batman and Robin arrived on the scene, the lab was engulfed in flames. What looked like Zone's remains were found in the ashes. Eventually, Clayface would return and bring chaos to the world.

WHOA!

SFX: CRASH

COULD THAT BE...

CLAY-FACE!!

MWA HA HA HA...

CLAYFACE, YOU FIEND! WHERE'D YOU GET THE BIOPLASM?
YOU MEAN THE ALIEN LIFE LIQUID?

ALIEN LIFE LIQUID...

THAT'S RIGHT, AND IT'S IN MY BODY...
...ENABLING ME TO CHANGE FORM WITH ITS POWERS.

SO YOU ATTACKED PROFESSOR ZONE TO GET YOUR HANDS ON IT.

HA HA HA... SHALL I DEMONSTRATE ITS POWER, BATMAN?

MONSTER!

SFX: FWISH

FOOL! DO YOU THINK THIS ROPE CAN HOLD ME?

BATMAN! HE'S MORPHING!

UNGH!

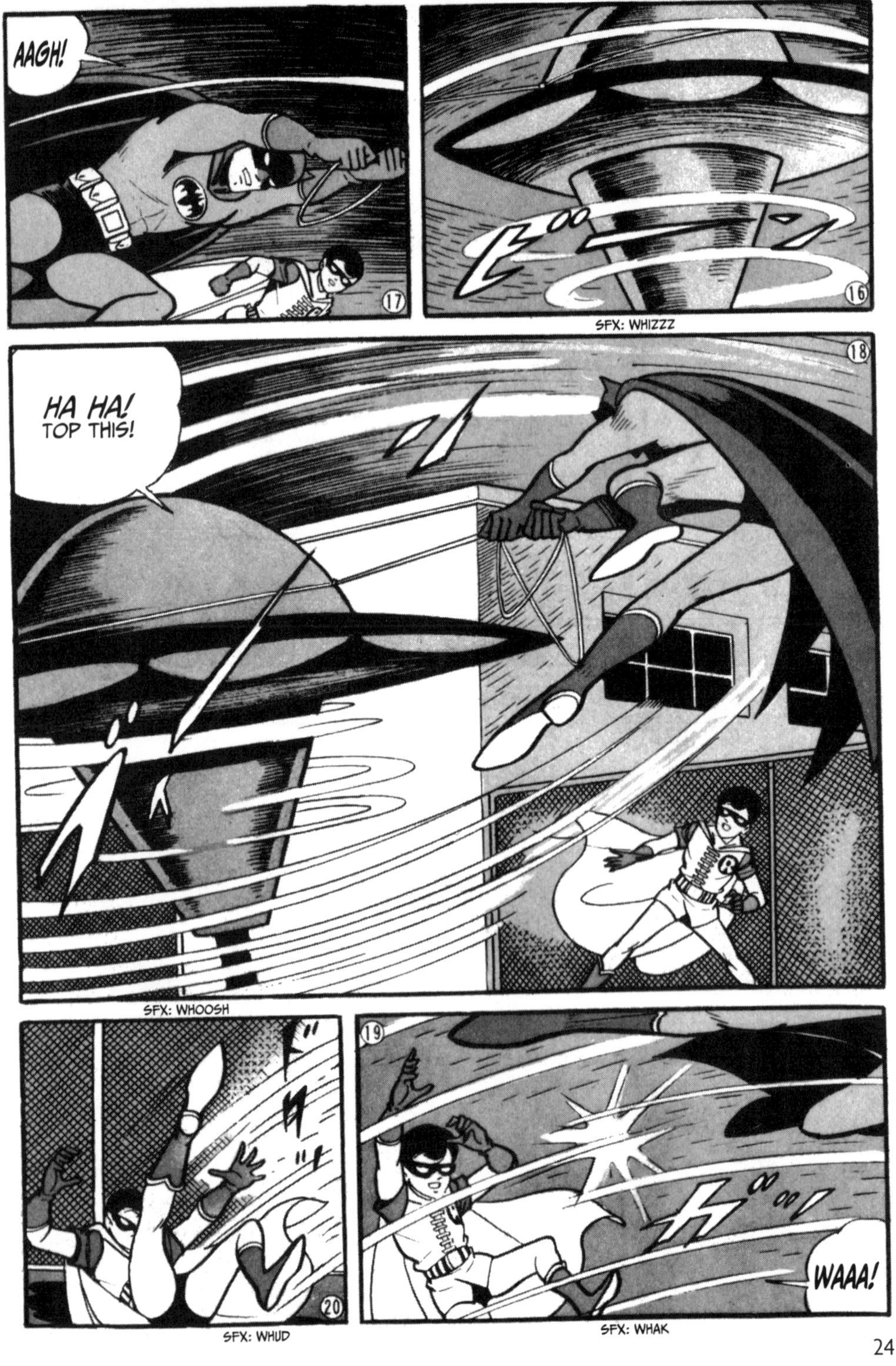

SFX: WHIZZZ

AAGH!

HA HA!
TOP THIS!

SFX: WHOOSH

WAAA!

SFX: WHAK

SFX: WHUD

SFX: WHIZZZ
WHAT INCREDIBLE CENTRIFUGAL FORCE!
SFX: WHOOSH
IF THIS KEEPS UP I'LL BE THROWN OFF AND SLAMMED INTO THE WALL!
WAIT! THERE'S A GAP IN THAT CHAIN-LINK FENCE.
SFX: FWOOSH
IF I CAN JUST TIME IT TO BE THROWN THROUGH THAT GAP...
SFX: WHIZZZ
IT'S MY ONLY WAY OUT. ALL RIGHT, IT'S SINK OR SWIM NOW...
ONE...
TWO....
THREE!!
SFX: FWOP
SFX: FWISH

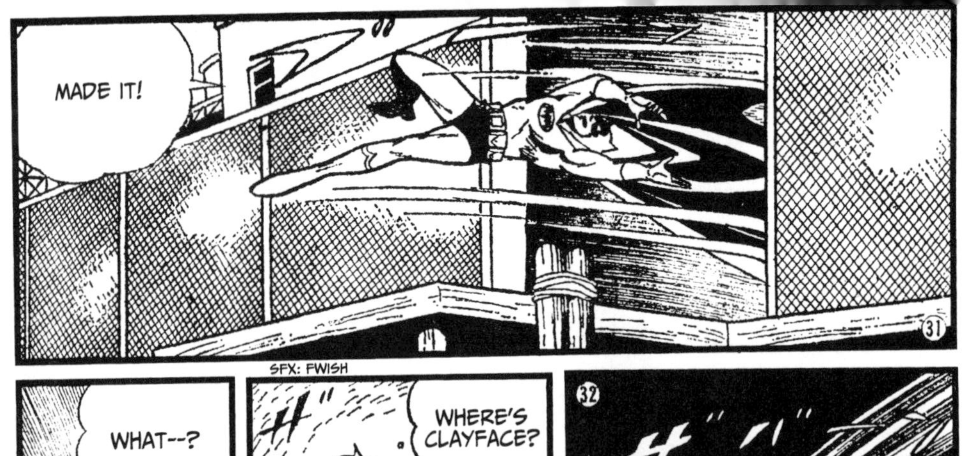
MADE IT!
31

SFX: FWISH

32

SFX: SPLOOSH

WHERE'S CLAYFACE?
33

SFX: SPLASH

WHAT--?
34

35

36

37

SFX: FLAP FLAP

HE'S TURNED INTO PEGASUS AND FLOWN AWAY!

...

BATMAN!
ROBIN! ARE YOU OKAY?

I'M FINE.
BUT CLAYFACE ESCAPED.

HMMM. WE HAVE ANOTHER TERRIBLE VILLAIN ON OUR HANDS.

HE MOST LIKELY ATTACKED PROFESSOR ZONE AND STOLE THE BIOPLASM.

UNTIL WE CATCH HIM, WE CAN'T LET UP OUR SEARCH FOR EVEN A DAY.

AND SO, BATMAN BEGAN HIS TIRELESS QUEST FOR THE EVIL CLAYFACE.

BY DAY...

BY NIGHT...

THROUGH RAIN...

AND WIND...

EVEN WHEN ROBIN FELL ASLEEP EXHAUSTED, BATMAN CONTINUED THE SEARCH WITHOUT REST...

=SIGH= IT'S ALREADY BEEN A WEEK...

CLAYFACE HASN'T APPEARED SINCE OUR LAST FIGHT. WHERE ON EARTH IS HE, AND WHAT'S HE SCHEMING?

SFX: RATTLE CRASH

SFX: SWISH

THAT NOISE! IT SOUNDED LIKE SOMEONE COLLAPSED.

BATMAN!

WHAT HAPPENED? ARE YOU ALL RIGHT?
UH...YES, IT'S NOTHING.

I'M JUST OVER-TIRED.

BUT OF COURSE YOU ARE--YOU HAVEN'T SLEPT A WINK IN A WEEK.

YOU SHOULD GO TO THE CLUB AND REST UP A LITTLE.
YES. I NEED TO CLEAR MY HEAD AND RECHARGE.

I'LL TAKE OVER THE SEARCH.

AND I'LL LET YOU KNOW IF ANYTHING HAPPENS.

THANKS, DICK. YOU DO THAT.

THIS IS THE PARRO CLUB, WHERE THE GENTLEMEN OF GOTHAM CITY COME TO RELAX AND SOCIALIZE.

HAVING LEFT THE SEARCH TO ROBIN, BATMAN RESUMES HIS SECRET IDENTITY AS BRUCE WAYNE IN ORDER TO REST UP.

WAYNE! IT'S BEEN A WHILE.
PHIPPS! HI THERE.

71
YOU'VE BEEN AWAY SO LONG...
I WANT TO INTRODUCE YOU TO A NEW CLUB MEMBER WHO JOINED WHILE YOU WERE GONE.

72
THIS IS COLT.

73
PLEASED TO MEET YOU.
LIKEWISE, MR. COLT.

BY THE WAY, WAYNE. DID I TELL YOU I BOUGHT ANOTHER MASTERPIECE?
OH?
74

IT'S A REMBRANDT AND BOY, IS IT SOMETHING.
WOW. I'D LIKE TO SEE THAT.
75

BUT BE CAREFUL. THAT VILLAIN CLAYFACE IS KNOWN TO HAVE AN EYE FOR ART. YOU NEVER KNOW, HE MIGHT TRY TO STEAL IT.
76

IT'S OKAY, I HAVEN'T TOLD ANYONE ABOUT IT YET.
I WANTED YOU TO BE THE FIRST ONE TO SEE IT.
77

WHY DON'T YOU COME BY TONIGHT AND HAVE A LOOK?
THANKS! I'LL DO THAT.
78

I CAN'T HELP WORRYING ABOUT ROBIN ON PATROL, EVEN HERE.
I'LL GO OUT TO THE LAWN AND CONTACT HIM.
SFX: SHIK
THIS IS BATMAN. BATMAN, OVER.
ROBIN, COME IN.
ANY NEWS?
ROBIN HERE.
NOTHING UNUSUAL.

BATMAN, DON'T YOU WORRY ABOUT ME. JUST TAKE IT EASY.
86

HEH. YOU KNOW ME, ALWAYS WORKING.
TALK TO YOU LATER.
87

WELL THEN, I GUESS IT'S OFF TO PHIPPS'S HOME FOR A VISIT.
88

89

フイプス
90

SIGN: PHIPPS

フイプス
91

SIGN: PHIPPS

BRUCE! IT'S YOU.
HI, PHIPPS. I'VE COME TO SEE THAT REMBRANDT OF YOURS.
92

O-OH! I'M SORRY, BUT I'VE GOT THIS AWFUL TOOTHACHE.
JUST TERRIBLE.
93

I DO APOLOGIZE, BUT COULD YOU COME BACK ANOTHER DAY?
SURE, NO PROBLEM.
94

TOOTHACHE, *EH?*

SFX: SWISH

THAT'S NOT PHIPPS...
PHIPPS WEARS A FULL SET OF DENTURES. HE DOESN'T ***HAVE*** ANY TEETH!

SOMEONE'S POSING AS HIM.
PROBABLY TO GET AT THAT PAINTING.

A-HA! HERE HE COMES.

AND HE'S CARRYING A PACKAGE.

HUH?!
SFX: SWOOP

UGH!

SFX: KRAK

B-BATMAN!

WHO ARE YOU REALLY? YOU'RE NOT GETTING AWAY WITH THAT PAINTING!

HA HA HA. YOU SAW THROUGH ME, *EH?*

SFX: DRIP DRIP

CLAYFACE! SO IT *IS* YOU!

MWA HA HA! YOU THINK YOU CAN CATCH ME?

バットマン
BATMAN
EXCLUSIVE
JAPANESE VERSION
SHONEN GAHOSHA
© N.P.P. 1966
★THE REVENGE OF CLAYFACE Part 3★
...HE'S TV'S MOST POPULAR STAR, BATMAN!!
WHETHER IN AMERICA OR JAPAN...
Jiro Kuwata

CLAYFACE HAS TURNED INTO A GHOST-BAT!

FIEND!

RAHHR!

AGH!
SFX: FLAP

SFX: WHUD

BOOMERANG TRANQUILIZER!

SFX: SHRIEK

SFX: SWISH

SFX: FWISH

HE DODGED IT!

ONE MORE!

SFX: FLAP

NOW WHAT?

A BEETLE!

I'LL PUT HIM TO SLEEP!

SFX: SWISH

SFX: CHAK

DRAT! BOUNCED OFF!

TAKE THIS!

SFX: SWISH SWISH

SFX: CHAK CHAK

MWA HA HA!
I'VE BEEN HIT BY THE BOOMERANG TRANQUILIZER BEFORE! DID YOU THINK I'D FALL FOR THAT AGAIN?

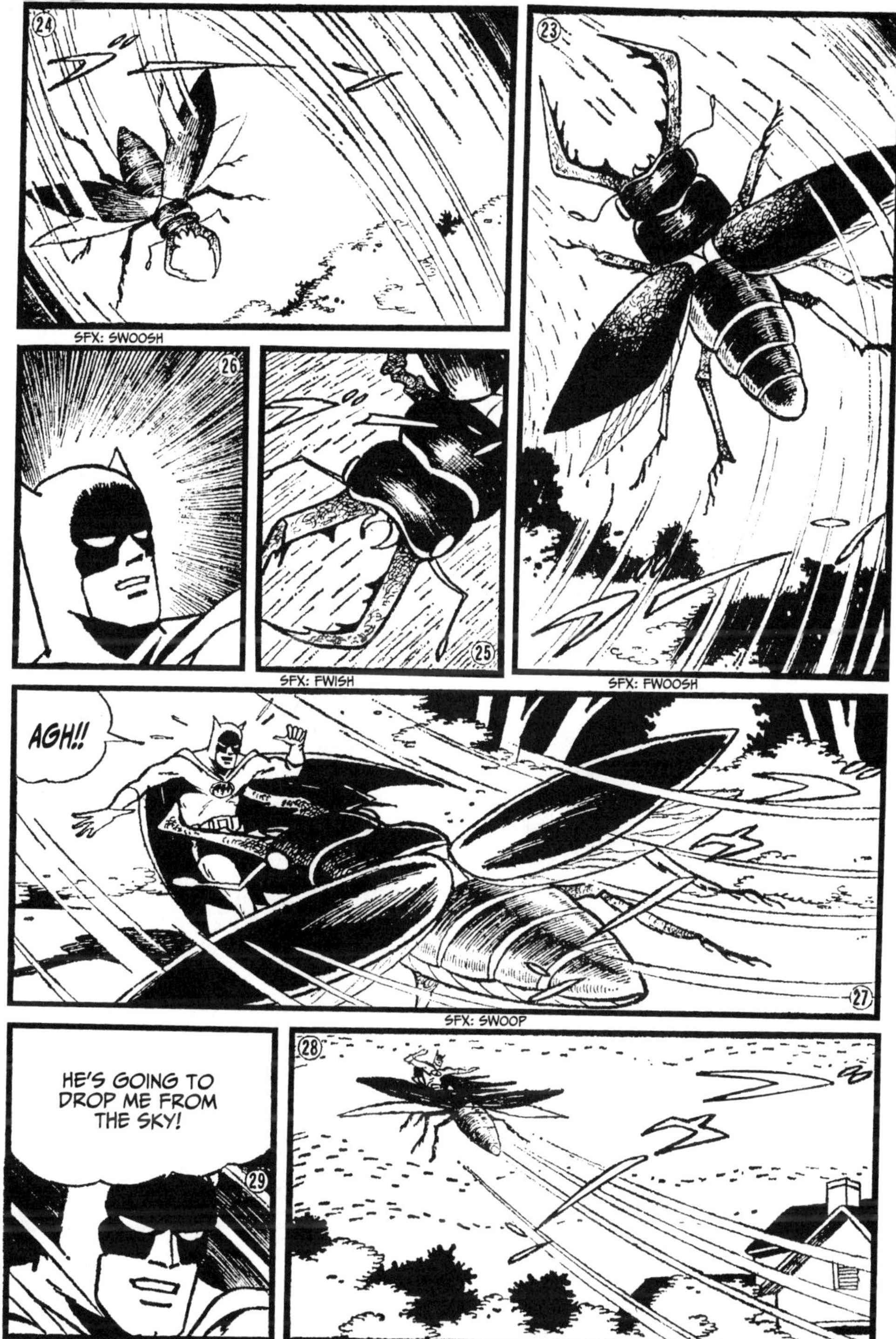

SFX: FWOOSH

SFX: SWOOSH

SFX: FWISH

AGH!!

SFX: SWOOP

SFX: WHOOSH

HE'S GOING TO DROP ME FROM THE SKY!

31
BON VOY-AGE!

THAT'S RIGHT. YOU'LL BE FLATTENED AND DIE!
30

32

DO YOU THINK THIS...
33

... IS ALL IT TAKES?
34

I'VE GOT MOVES LIKE *THIS*, TOO.
35

SFX: FWOO

37

SFX: SKREEE

ROBIN!
36

SFX: VRRR

BATMAN! YOU WEREN'T RESPONDING TO MY CALLS, SO I CAME HERE MYSELF. WHAT'S HAPPENED?
38

IT'S CLAYFACE.
WHAT? HE'S TURNED UP?
39

40
THE BOOMERANG TRANQUILIZER DIDN'T STOP HIM AND HE GOT AWAY.

BUT FIRST LET'S CHECK ON PHIPPS. I HOPE HE'S ALL RIGHT!
41

42

SFX: KA-CHA

BATMAN!
WHEW! YOU'RE ONLY TIED UP. THANK GOODNESS.

THAT AWFUL CLAYFACE DISGUISED HIMSELF AS ME...
AND THEN MADE OFF WITH MY PRECIOUS ART!

JUST WAIT AND SEE. I PROMISE TO FIGURE OUT A WAY TO BRING CLAYFACE DOWN!
AND I'LL GET BACK YOUR PAINTING.

HOW ON EARTH ARE WE GOING TO CAPTURE HIM?

THE BOOMERANG AND THE TRANQ DIDN'T WORK...
WHAT ABOUT A RIFLE?

THAT WOULDN'T WORK, EITHER.
HE CAN TRANSFORM HIMSELF INTO A ROCK OR SOMETHING AND THE BULLETS WILL JUST BOUNCE OFF.

PILING ONTO HIM WON'T DO IT.

NEITHER WILL HITTING HIM...

IS THERE NO OTHER WAY?
UM... UM...

BATMAN!
IT'S THE BAT-PHONE!

SFX: BEEP BEEP

HELLO, INSPECTOR GORDON?
THIS IS NO TIME FOR "HELLO," BATMAN!

CLAYFACE HAS JUST HIT THREE MORE LOCATIONS!

WHAT HAPPENED?

ALL OF THEM WERE ROBBED OF PRECIOUS ARTWORK!

WHO EXACTLY WAS ATTACKED?

A BUSINESSMAN NAMED GARY SMITH, A TRADING MERCHANT NAMED JIM COTTON, AND A POLITICIAN NAMED CHURCHILL BARR.

THEY'RE ALL MEMBERS OF THE PARRO CLUB!

UGH--I JUST WANT TO RUN TO THE NORTH POLE OR SOMETHING WHILE CLAYFACE WREAKS HAVOC!

THE NORTH POLE?!

ARE YOU LISTENING? HELLO? BATMAN?!

THAT'S IT! THE NORTH POLE!
HELLO? HELLO?!

ROBIN, I THINK I HAVE THE ANSWER.
WHA--?

THE NORTH POLE! A GLACIER!

GLACIER? WHAT ARE YOU GOING TO DO?

PREPARE THE FREEZER GUN!

THAT WAY THERE'S NO GRAPPLING. WE CAN JUST FREEZE HIM.
I SEE...

ONE MORE THING. EVERYONE WHO'S BEEN ATTACKED IS IN THE PARRO CLUB...

AND THE CRIMES STARTED TAKING PLACE ONLY WHEN THIS MAN "COLT" BECAME A NEW MEMBER...

SO THIS COLT GUY COULD BE CLAYFACE!

WE DON'T KNOW THAT FOR SURE.
WE NEED TO INVESTIGATE.

FIRST, LET'S GO SEE COLT.
WHAT ABOUT THE FREEZER GUN?

NOT YET. I WANT TO ESTABLISH HIS IDENTITY.

SFX: VROOOO

SFX: NOK NOK

IT'S LOCKED.
HE MUST NOT
BE HOME.

THAT'S GOOD.
WE CAN SEARCH
THE HOUSE.

WINDOW'S
OPEN.

=GASP!=

COLT!
MMGGG--

WHAT HAPPENED?
MMGGG--

CLAYFACE CAME AND STOLE MY ART!
WHAT?

IT HAPPENED JUST NOW! HURRY! HE WENT OUT THE BACK!

LET'S GO, ROBIN!

にやり
SFX: SNEER

IDIOTS! I KNEW AS SOON AS THE BATMOBILE PULLED UP THAT I WAS UNDER SUSPICION, SO I TIED MYSELF UP.

93
JUST AS BATMAN SUSPECTED...

I AM WHO HE THINKS I AM.
94

BUT HE CAN'T BE SURE OF THAT YET.
95

I NEED TO SHOW BATMAN AND ROBIN THE CLAYFACE WHO ATTACKED MR. COLT.
96

I MUST HEAD THEM OFF.
97

IT'S SHOWTIME!
98

99

SFX: SSSSSSS

BATMAN! WHERE'S CLAYFACE?
100

WHAT'S THAT?

SFX: SSSSSS

GASP!

BATMAN! IT'S A GIANT SNAKE!

GIANT SNAKES SHOULD *NOT* BE HERE.
SO...

MWA HA HA HA!

IT'S CLAYFACE!

SFX: DRIP DRIP

LOOK OUT!

SFX: WHUNK

SFX: RATTLE RATTLE

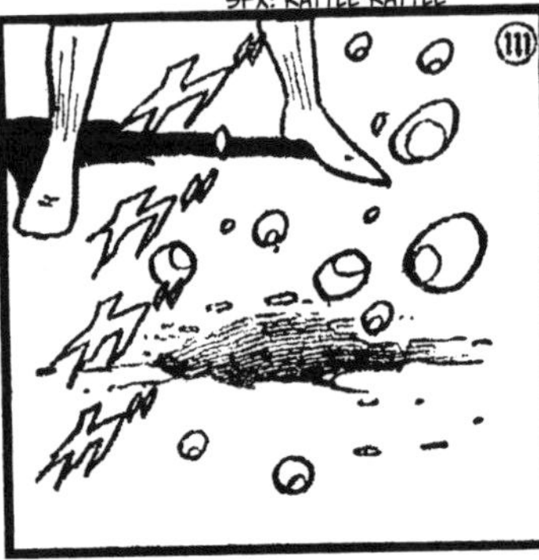

SFX: RATTLE RATTLE

MWA HA HA HA HA! GIVE UP TRYING TO CATCH ME, BATMAN! I'M UNCATCHABLE!

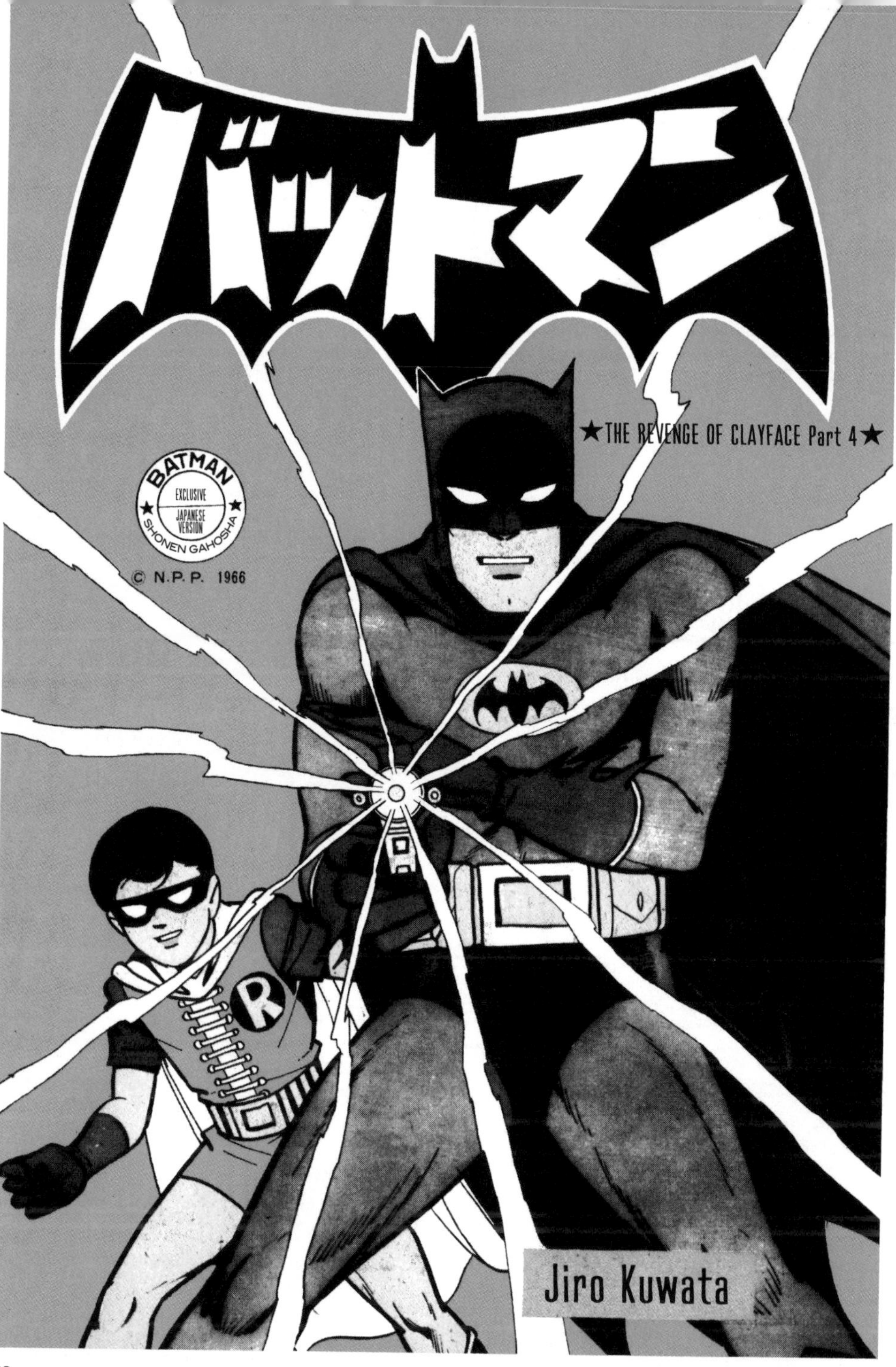
バットマン
★THE REVENGE OF CLAYFACE Part 4★
BATMAN
EXCLUSIVE
JAPANESE VERSION
SHONEN GAHOSHA
© N.P.P. 1966
Jiro Kuwata

LAST EPISODE...

Batman and Robin suspected Colt of being Clayface and headed for his house. But they were attacked by Clayface there, while Colt was bound and gagged! However, it was only a ruse, with Colt playing the victim card to throw off suspicion...

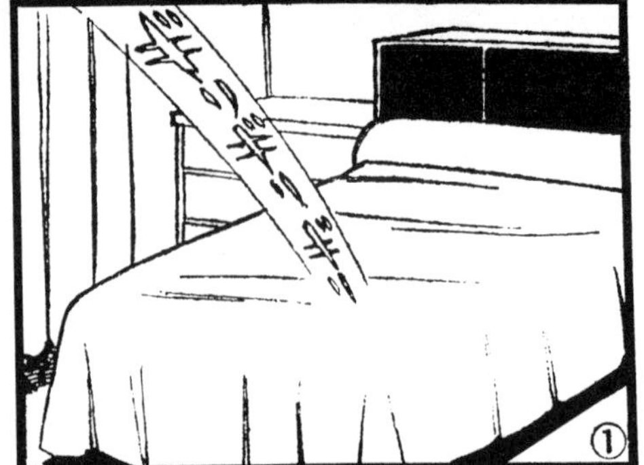

SFX: FSSSS

SFX: FSS FSS

SFX: BLOOP BLOOP

CHUCKLE... AFTER I GET THROUGH THIS, BATMAN WILL NEVER SUSPECT ME OF BEING CLAYFACE.

OH, BATMAN. DID YOU CATCH CLAYFACE?

UNFORTUNATELY, HE GOT AWAY.

I-I SEE. THE MAN'S A FIEND. I WAS TOTALLY NUMB WHEN YOU FOUND ME.

MR. COLT, I'D LIKE TO GET MORE DETAILS ABOUT THE ATTACK ON YOU.

WOULD YOU ACCOMPANY US TO THE POLICE STATION?
EH?

CURSE YOU, BATMAN! DO YOU SUSPECT ME AFTER ALL?

BUT APPEARING TO BE AFRAID OF THE POLICE WILL MAKE ME LOOK EVEN MORE SUSPICIOUS.

OF COURSE I'LL GO WITH YOU. IF MY ORDEAL CAN HELP THE INVESTIGATION, I'LL BE DELIGHTED.

ゴッタム警察署
けいさつしょ
SIGN: GOTHAM POLICE STATION

ANYWAY, HE APPEARED OUT OF NOWHERE...

ALL OF A SUDDEN, THIS WEIRD MUD BUBBLED UP INTO A HUMAN FORM.
I SEE...

AND THAT'S WHAT IT WAS LIKE WHEN CLAYFACE ATTACKED ME.

SORRY I MISSED OUT.
MR. COLT WAS JUST TELLING US ABOUT HIS MISFORTUNE, CHIEF GORDON.

MR. COLT, IF YOU WOULD, PLEASE SHARE YOUR STORY WITH ME, TOO.

HUH? TELL YOU THE SAME THING?

I DETAILED THE ENTIRE ENCOUNTER TO BATMAN.
HE CAN TELL YOU WHAT I SAID.
THE ONLY THING ...

WE HAVE TO GET GOING RIGHT AWAY. WE HAVE SOME BUSINESS TO ATTEND TO, MR. COLT.

SORRY, BUT FILL CHIEF GORDON IN ON WHAT HAPPENED AS WELL.
SEE YOU!

SFX: SHUT

MY GUT TELLS ME THAT COLT IS CLAYFACE!

CLAYFACE CAN ONLY CHANGE HIS FORM FOR A LIMITED AMOUNT OF TIME.

AFTER THE TIME'S UP, THE EFFECTIVENESS OF THE ALIEN LIFE LIQUID WILL WEAR OFF AND HE'LL RETURN TO HIS ORIGINAL FORM.

THEN YOU'RE TRYING TO BUY TIME SO WE CAN SEE COLT'S TRUE IDENTITY WITH OUR OWN EYES.

COME ON, LET'S PREPARE A FREEZE GUN IN THE MEANTIME.
GOOD PLAN.

ALL RIGHT, MR. COLT.

...

I APOLOGIZE, BUT PLEASE GIVE ME ALL THE DETAILS.
FINE... AS YOU LIKE.

AND THEN CLAYFACE APPEARED...
MM-HM... AND THEN?

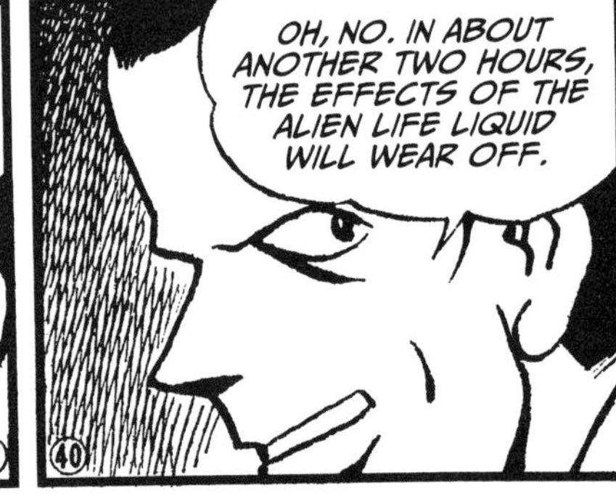
OH, NO. IN ABOUT ANOTHER TWO HOURS, THE EFFECTS OF THE ALIEN LIFE LIQUID WILL WEAR OFF.

AND IF THAT HAPPENS, I'LL RETURN TO MY ORIGINAL FORM.

AND THEN WHAT HAPPENED, MR. COLT?

S-SO THEN, CLAYFACE...
MM-HM...

THEN BATMAN ARRIVED...

GRRR... JUST ONE HOUR LEFT...

UM... WHERE DID, UH, CLAYFACE APPEAR EXACTLY AGAIN, MR. COLT?

HOW MANY TIMES ARE YOU GOING TO MAKE ME REPEAT MYSELF?!
SFX: BAM

OH, THAT'S RIGHT. I ASKED YOU THAT BEFORE.
UM... THEN...

JUST 30 MINUTES. THIS IS BAD... SOMEHOW, I'VE GOT TO GET OUT OF HERE!

WHAT'S THIS? MR. COLT, YOU LOOK GREEN ABOUT THE GILLS. AND YOU'RE DRIPPING SWEAT!
UM...

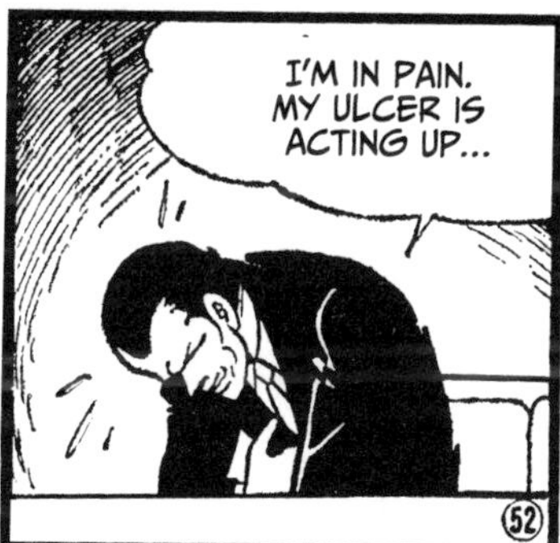
I'M IN PAIN. MY ULCER IS ACTING UP...

53
YOUR ULCER?! WE CAN'T HAVE THAT!

54
JUST LET ME GO HOME AND REST.

55
OH, NO, WE'D BETTER GET YOU TO A HOSPITAL! THERE'S ONE RIGHT OVER THERE! I'LL TAKE YOU MYSELF!

56
N-NO THANK YOU! I'VE GOT MEDICATION AT HOME...

57
SFX:SLAM

58
SFX: BEEP BEEP

59
BATMAN! THE ALARM!
RIGHT!
SFX: BEEP BEEP

60
HI, BATMAN. COLT JUST FEIGNED ILLNESS AND LEFT.
THAT RAT! THE EFFECTS OF THE ALIEN LIFE LIQUID MUST HAVE WORN OFF.

61
I COULDN'T LEGALLY PREVENT HIM FROM LEAVING...
...SO THE REST IS UP TO YOU!

ROBIN, TO THE BATMOBILE!
WE'LL GET A HEAD START ON COLT'S DESTINATION AND NAB HIM THERE!
SFX: WHOOOSH
SFX: ZOOOM
SEVEN MORE MINUTES!

THE HOUSE IS IN SIGHT AT LAST!

ONE MORE MINUTE!

SFX: FWISH

B-BATMAN!
HI, MR. COLT!

THERE'S SOMETHING I FORGOT TO ASK, SO WE'VE BEEN WAITING FOR YOU HERE.

OH, NO! I'M OUT OF TIME...

75
JUST ONE QUESTION...

76
WAIT! MY ULCER IS KILLING ME!

77
LET ME TAKE MY MEDICINE FIRST.
THEN WE'LL TALK!

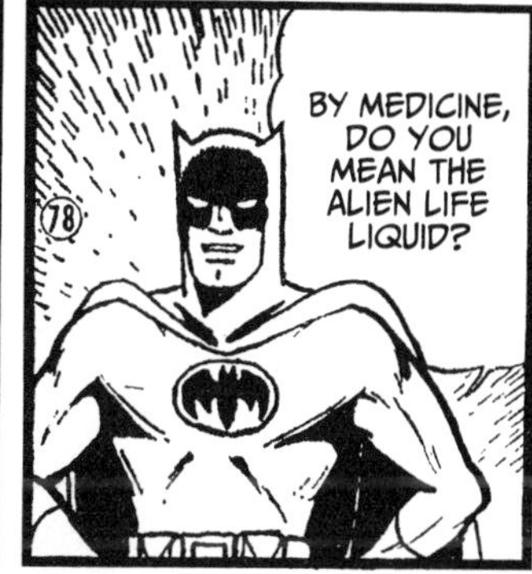
78
BY MEDICINE, DO YOU MEAN THE ALIEN LIFE LIQUID?

79
W-WHAT?!

80
LET'S SEE WHO YOU REALLY ARE, COLT!
I ALREADY KNOW YOU'RE CLAYFACE!

81
ULP...

82

83

84
AH! PROFESSOR ZONE!

85
I WAS SO SURE CLAYFACE WAS STILL FERRIS...
...BUT IT WAS YOU, PROFESSOR ZONE?!

86
HMPH! AFTER MY RESIDENCE BURNED DOWN, A CHARRED CORPSE WAS FOUND AMONG THE EMBERS, RIGHT?
THAT WAS FERRIS!

AFTER THAT, I TOOK HIS PLACE AS CLAYFACE AND WENT ON A RAMPAGE!

BUT WHY WOULD YOU DO SOMETHING SO EVIL, PROFESSOR?

HMPH. LOOK HOW OLD I AM! I DON'T WANT TO END MY LIFE AS A POOR SCHOLAR...
I'M GOING TO ENJOY THE REST OF MY DAYS USING THE ALIEN LIFE LIQUID!

AND YOU'D BEST NOT GET IN MY WAY!

SFX: SLAM

PROFESSOR, WAIT!

UNGH... HE'S LOCKED IT.

OKAY, I'LL JUST BREAK IT DOWN.

SFX: THUD THUD THUD

SFX: CRASH

AH!
SFX: STICK

CHUCKLE...
IF YOU TWO INSIST ON INTERFERING, THEN YOUR LIVES ARE FORFEIT.

HMM... THE PROFESSOR MUST'VE QUICKLY INJECTED HIMSELF, THEN TURNED INTO THE FORM OF A GIANT SPIDER!

MIS-CREANT!

SFX: FOOSH

AAAAH!

WAAA!

SFX: SPLEK

DRAT! THESE STRINGS ARE SO STICKY THAT I CAN BARELY MOVE!

I'VE GOT IT! FIRST, I'LL BURN THE STRANDS WITH MY FIRE PISTOL.

SFX: FSSSS

IT'S WORKING! THE STRINGS ARE MELTING!

B-BATMAN!

NOW COOL DOWN WITH MY FREEZE GUN!

SFX: BEE-BEE-BEE-BEE

SFX: BEE-BEE-BEE-BEE-BEE

SFX: THUD

SUCCESS! NOW I'LL MELT MORE STRINGS TO GET YOU DOWN, ROBIN!

SFX: FSSSS

WHEN THE PROFESSOR TURNS BACK TO NORMAL, HE'LL FIND HIMSELF IN A JAIL CELL.

IT'S A SHAME. IF HE HADN'T FOLLOWED THROUGH ON ONE STUPID IDEA, HE WOULD'VE LIVED THE REST OF HIS LIFE AS A WELL-RESPECTED, FINE CHEMIST.

バットマン
★THE HANGMAN OF TERROR★
Jiro Kuwata

AND NOW, TODAY'S MAIN EVENT!

SFX: WAAAAA WAAAA

IN THE RED CORNER, APACHE ARROW!

SFX: WAAAA WAAAA

AND HIS OPPONENT, IN THE BLUE CORNER, THE HANGMAN!

SFX: OOOO OOO

BRUCE, ALL OF A SUDDEN, THE HANGMAN'S A SUPERSTAR. I HEAR HE HASN'T LOST EVEN ONE BOUT!
YES, WELL, HE DOES LOOK TO BE A VERY STRONG PRO WRESTLER.

IF APACHE ARROW WINS THIS MATCH...

...HE'LL TEAR OFF THE HANGMAN'S HOOD!

YAAA!
YOU CAN DO IT, APACHE ARROW!
YEAH! RIP OFF THE HANGMAN'S HOOD!

SFX: WAAA WAAA

IT SOUNDS LIKE EVERYONE'S ROOTING FOR APACHE ARROW.

THE HANGMAN'S STRONG BUT HE FIGHTS DIRTY, SO HE'S PRETTY MUCH DESPISED, APPARENTLY.

THAT'S WHY THE CROWD IS HOPING TO SEE APACHE WIN AND THE HANGMAN GET DE-HOODED.

SFX: CLANG

SFX: GRAB

ARRHH!

UNGH!

THAT'S APACHE ARROW'S HAMMER THROW.

SFX: WHUMP

SFX: THUD THUD THUD

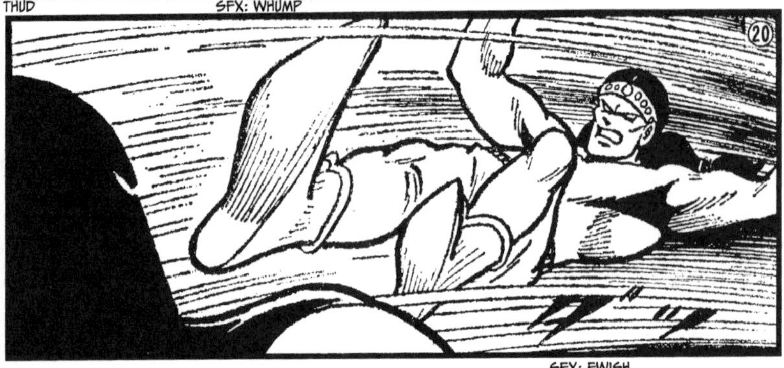
SFX: FWISH

THERE IT IS! THE FLYING APACHE ARROW!

SFX: KRAK

AH! THE HANGMAN DEFLECTED THE ARROW KICK!

SFX: YANK

SFX: WOK

SEE? THAT WAS AGAINST THE RULES.

THAT WAS LOW, HANGMAN!
KNOCK IT OFF!

SFX: WHUD WHUD WHUD

THE REFEREE HAS STARTED THE COUNT. IF FIVE SECONDS PASS, THE HANGMAN WILL BE DISQUALIFIED!

ONE! TWO!

THREE! FOUR!

SFX: SLUMP

SFX: SWISH

THE HANGMAN FINALLY GAVE UP ON HIS ILLEGAL HOLD.
BUT APACHE ARROW IS STAGGERING!

HEH...

I WONDER IF APACHE ARROW CAN STILL FIGHT...

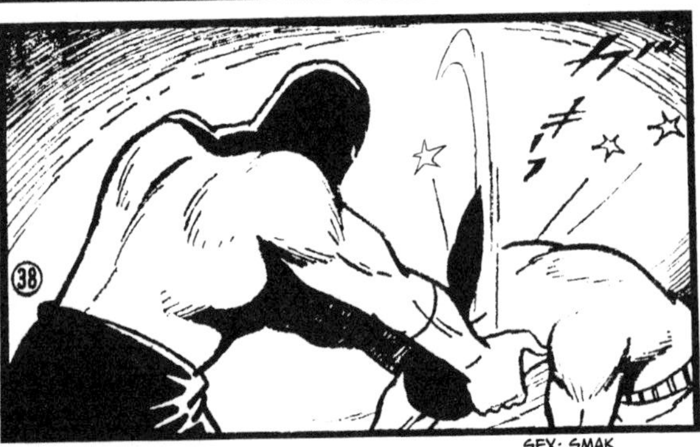

SFX: SMAK

SFX: SPIN

AH! THERE IT IS! THE HANGING!
APACHE ARROW IS IN A REAL PINCH!

URK...

APACHE, FIGHT BACK!
SHAKE YOURSELF FREE!
HE'LL MURDER YOU!

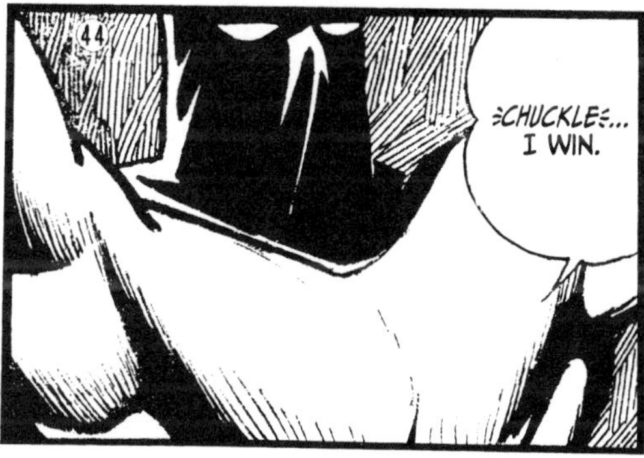
≈CHUCKLE≈... I WIN.

SFX: WOK

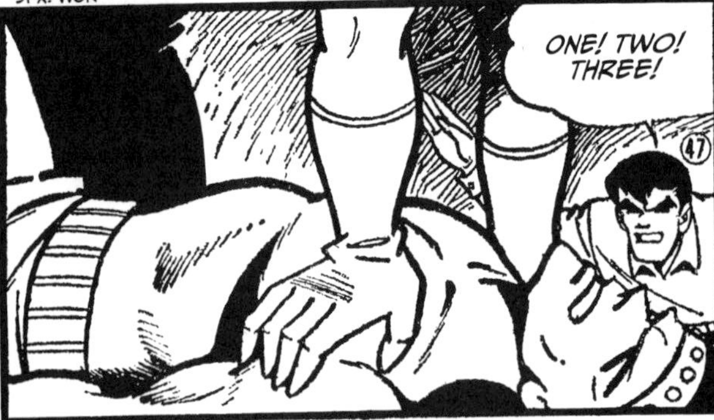
ONE! TWO! THREE!

AND THAT BRINGS THIS BOUT TO A QUICK CLOSE.
APACHE ARROW WAS NO MATCH FOR THE HANGMAN, EITHER.

HANGMAN, YOU'RE A JERK!
WHY DON'T YA GO HANG YOURSELF?!

50
SO APACHE ARROW DIDN'T WIN EITHER, *EH?*

AND SO WE STILL DON'T KNOW THE IDENTITY OF THE HANGMAN.
51

WHY DON'T WE LOOK INTO WHO HE REALLY IS?
52

HAHAHA. NO DICE, DICK.
WE CAN'T SLACK OFF ON OUR PATROLS TO KEEP THE PEACE OF GOTHAM CITY JUST TO SATISFY OUR OWN CURIOSITY.
53

54
AND SPEAKING OF WHICH, THE SUN IS STARTING TO GO DOWN...
LET'S BEGIN OUR PATROL IN THE BATMOBILE!

56

AH!

B-BATMAN!

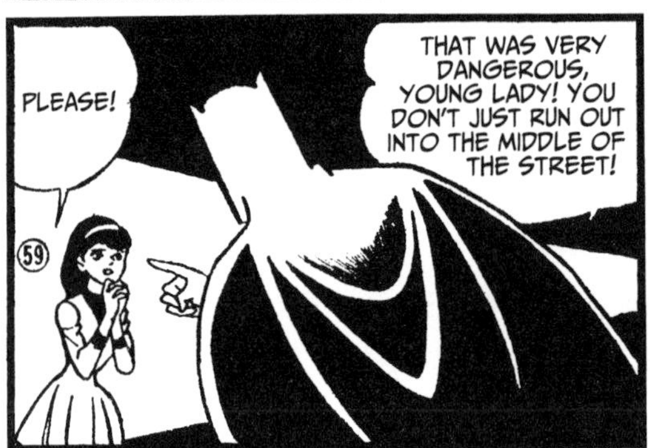
THAT WAS VERY DANGEROUS, YOUNG LADY! YOU DON'T JUST RUN OUT INTO THE MIDDLE OF THE STREET!
PLEASE!

I WAS WAITING FOR YOU TWO TO COME THIS WAY WHILE ON PATROL.
WHAT DO YOU WANT?

PLEASE HELP MY BIG BROTHER!

HUH? YOUR BIG BROTHER?

HE'S GOING TO COMMIT A CRIME!
PLEASE STOP HIM!

WHAT DO YOU MEAN?

THERE'S NO TIME TO EXPLAIN!
PLEASE, JUST HURRY OVER TO PEARL JEWELERS!

66
I CAN TELL FROM THE GIRL'S FACE THAT THIS IS NO TRIVIAL MATTER...
ALL RIGHT, LET'S GO, ROBIN!

67
SFX: WHOOSH

68
SFX: WHIZZZ

69
WHERE IS PEARL JEWELERS?

70
ON 3RD STREET!

71
SFX: WHIZZZ

72
THERE IT IS!

73
AH! THE JEWELRY STORE'S BURGLAR ALARM IS GOING OFF!
SFX: RING RING RING RING RING

SIGN: JEWELER SFX: RING RING RING

HURRY, ROBIN!

SFX: CRASH

AH! IT'S THE HANGMAN!

SFX: CLACK CLACK CLACK

HALT!

SFX: TA TA TA
SFX: CLACK CLACK CLACK
SFX: CLACK CLACK CLACK
THERE! HE'S GOING UP THE EMERGENCY STAIRS!
SFX: CLACK CLACK CLACK

88

SFX: FWISH

89

AH! ANOTHER HANGMAN ON THE ROOF, BATMAN!
90

91

SFX: SLAP

AAAH!
92

SFX: HOIST

93

AH!
94

95

SFX: SPLAT

ONE HANGMAN THREW THE OTHER OFF THE ROOF!
WHAT THE DEVIL IS GOING ON HERE?!
96

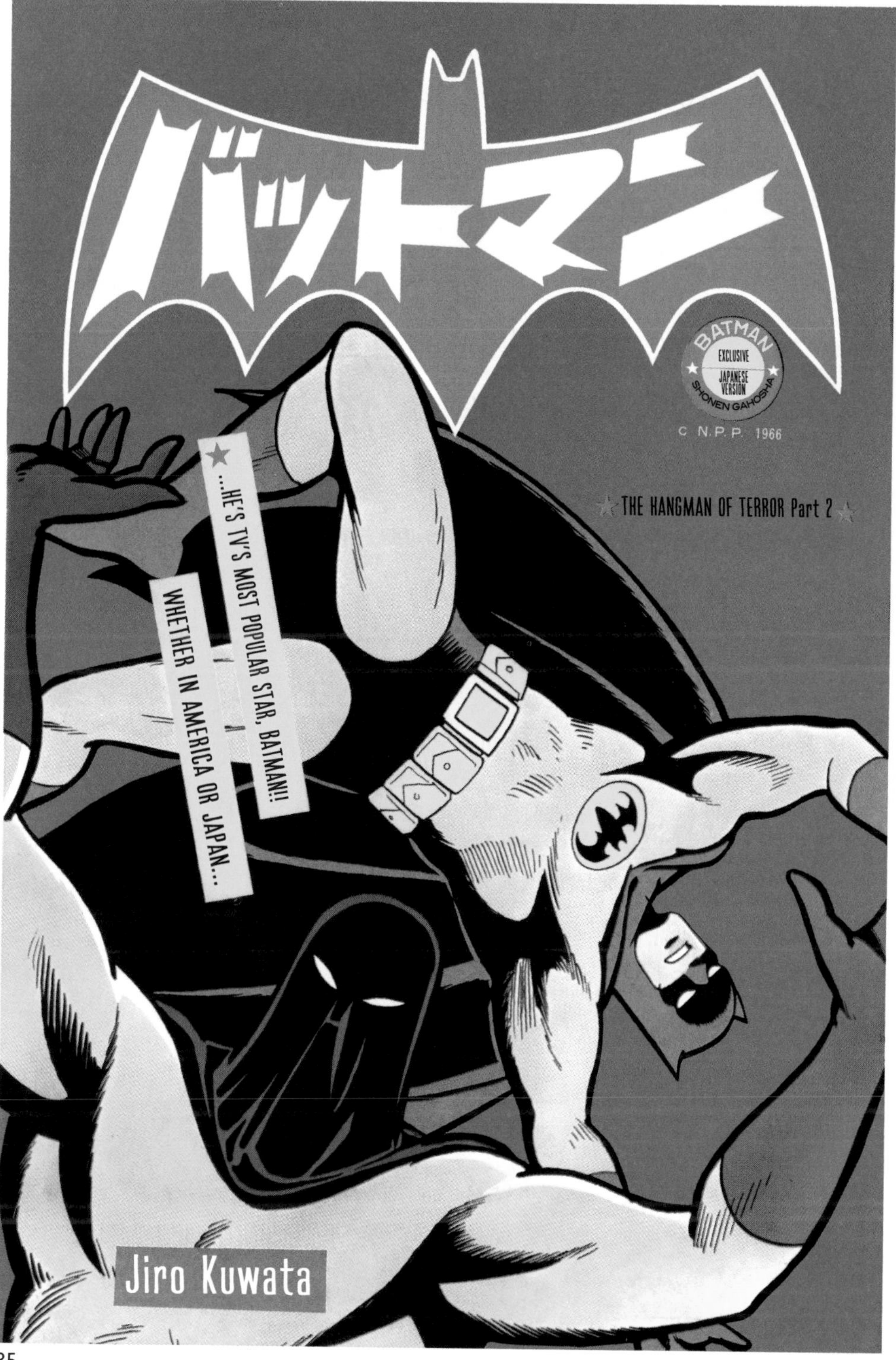
バットマン
BATMAN
EXCLUSIVE
JAPANESE VERSION
SHONEN GAHOSHA
C N.P.P. 1966
THE HANGMAN OF TERROR Part 2
WHETHER IN AMERICA OR JAPAN...
...HE'S TV'S MOST POPULAR STAR, BATMAN!!
Jiro Kuwata

SFX: SPLAT

LAST EPISODE...

While Batman and Robin were on patrol at night, a girl ran in front of the Batmobile and cried, "Batman! My big brother is about to commit a crime! Hurry over to Pearl Jewelers and help him!" When the Dynamic Duo rushed over to the jewelry store, they found pro wrestling bad guy, the Hangman!

AH! THE HANGMAN GOT THROWN OFF THE ROOF!

A-AND THE ONE WHO THREW HIM OFF WAS ANOTHER HANGMAN!

WAHA HAHAHA HA...

TWO HANGMEN... WHAT DOES THIS MEAN?

LOOK!
THAT'S THE END OF THE MAN WHO IMPERSONATED ME TO DO EVIL!

BATMAN, YOU CAN DEAL WITH THE CORPSE!

WAIT! YOU OWE US AN EXPLANATION.

WAHAHAHA! ALL I DID WAS TAKE OUT A MURDERING BURGLAR! *TA-TA!*

NOT HERE?! HE VANISHED...

AH! BATMAN! DOWN THERE!
WHAT?

THE GIRL WHO CLUED US IN THAT SOMETHING WAS GOING TO HAPPEN...

SHE'S CRYING BESIDE THE DEAD BURG-LAR...

COME TO THINK OF IT, SHE SAID HER BROTHER WAS ABOUT TO COMMIT A CRIME AND WANTED US TO STOP HIM BEFOREHAND.

ROBIN! LET'S GET DOWN THERE. MAYBE THAT GIRL CAN SHED LIGHT ON THIS WHOLE MESS!

WHA...?! THE GIRL...

NOW SHE'S GONE...

I GUESS THIS BURGLAR IS THE OLDER BROTHER SHE WAS TALKING ABOUT.

MAYBE...

ANYWAY, TAKING THE HOOD OFF SHOULD GIVE US SOME ANSWERS...

WHY, THAT'S TIGER KID, THE PRO WRESTLER WHO RECENTLY RETIRED!

APPARENTLY, HE HIT HIS HEAD HARD DURING A MATCH AND HAS NEVER BEEN THE SAME SINCE.

BUT WAS HE IN FINANCIAL DISTRESS AND FINALLY DRESSED UP AS THE HANGMAN TO COMMIT A ROBBERY?

ゴッタム警察署
DAMNED PRO WRESTLING ROBBER!
HE KILLED TWO OF PEARL JEWELERS' NIGHT WATCHMEN WITH HIS BARE HANDS!

SIGN: GOTHAM POLICE STATION

BUT IN THE END, HE DIED AFTER THE HANGMAN THREW HIM OFF THE ROOF...
WELL, AT LEAST THE STOLEN GEMS WERE RECOVERED...

THE HANGMAN WHO KILLED THE ROBBER IS ALL OVER THE NEWSPAPERS.

BURGLAR IMPERSONATES THE HANGMAN... ROBS JEWELRY STORE...
BUT THEN THE REAL HANGMAN APPEARS, THEY BRAWL ON THE ROOF, AND FINALLY, THE MURDEROUS IMPOSTOR IS THROWN TO HIS DEATH, *EH?*

BUT SOMETHING DOESN'T ADD UP HERE...
WHAT DOESN'T?

FIRST OF ALL, THAT GIRL... TIGER KID DOESN'T HAVE A LITTLE SISTER.

SO WHO'S THE BIG BROTHER SHE WAS TALKING ABOUT?

THE GIRL WAS CRYING BESIDE THE CORPSE, BUT WHEN WE GOT DOWN TO STREET LEVEL, SHE WAS GONE.

AND I THINK IT'S STRANGE THAT THE HANGMAN SUDDENLY SHOWED UP ON THAT ROOF!

IT'S LIKE HE ALREADY KNEW ABOUT THE ROBBERY AND THE ESCAPE ROUTE THE THIEF WAS GOING TO TAKE.

BUT THE PEOPLE ARE TREATING THE HANGMAN LIKE A HERO FOR RIDDING THE CITY OF A ROBBER.

A HERO, *EH?*

ROBIN, I WANT YOU TO TRACK DOWN THAT GIRL IN TOWN.

I'LL SEE WHAT I CAN DO TO FIND OUT THE HANGMAN'S IDENTITY.
OKAY!

SFX: CHEER CHEER CHEER CHEER CHEER

HANGMAN! GOOD LUCK!
STARTING TODAY, I'M A FAN!

IN THE RED CORNER, THE HANGMAN!

IN THE BLUE CORNER, MAMMOTH RED!

MAMMOTH, YOU'LL NEVER UNMASK THE HANGMAN!
HANG 'IM, HANGMAN!

CHUCKLE...

THIS IS A SURPRISE. JUST THE OTHER DAY, THE CROWD SAW THE HANGMAN AS THE ENEMY...
...BUT AFTER THE ROBBERY INCIDENT, IT'S JUST THE OPPOSITE.

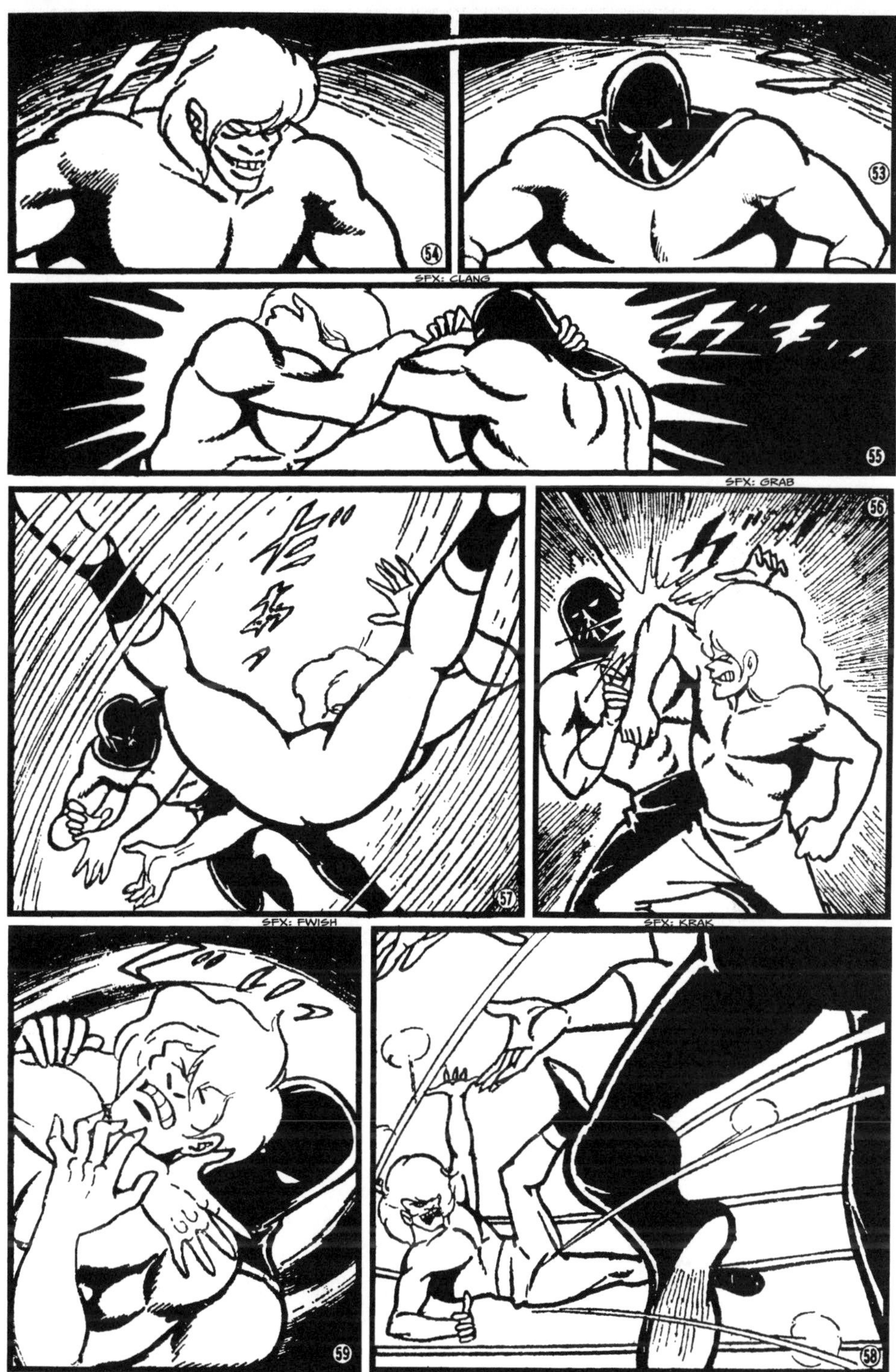
SFX: CLANG
SFX: GRAB
SFX: KRAK
SFX: FWISH
SFX: SQUEEZE

UNGH...

THERE'S NO HOPE FOR MAMMOTH NOW!
YEAH! THE HANGMAN'S SIGNATURE MOVE!

SFX: WHOOM

1! 2! 3!

THE HANGMAN WON TODAY, TOO. GUESS I DON'T HAVE MUCH CHANCE OF SEEING HIM UNMASKED THIS WAY...

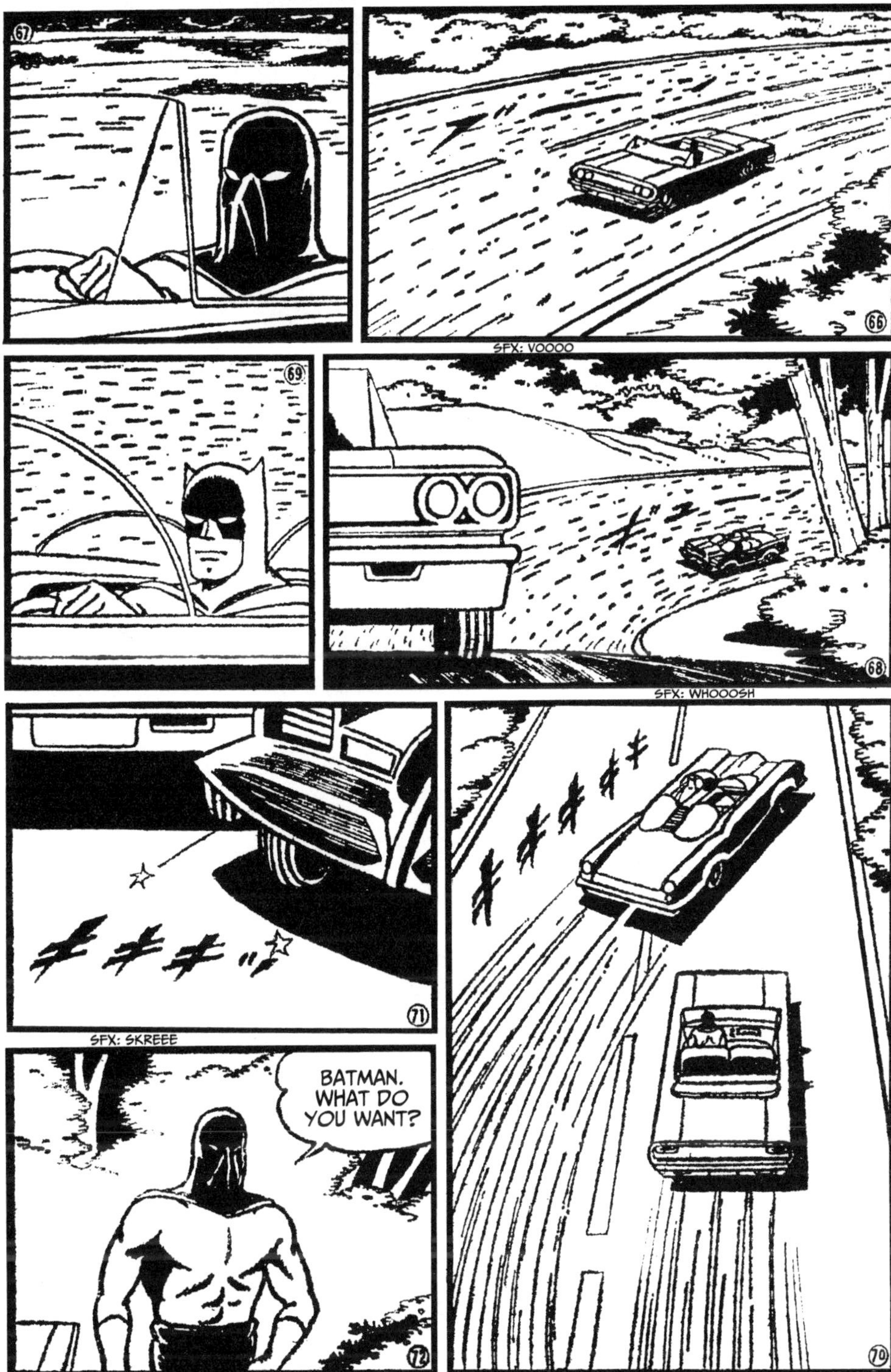
SFX: VOOOO
SFX: WHOOOSH
SFX: SKREEEE
SFX: SKREEE
BATMAN. WHAT DO YOU WANT?

I'VE GOT A REQUEST, HANGMAN.

TAKE OFF THAT HOOD!

TAKE OFF MY HOOD, YOU SAY?

WAHAHA HAHA!

THIS HOOD WILL ONLY COME OFF WHEN SOMEONE BEATS ME IN A MATCH.

ALL RIGHT, THEN, LET ME ASK YOU A QUESTION.
ON THE NIGHT OF THE ROBBERY, WHY WERE YOU ON THE SCENE?

HMPH! SO THAT'S WHAT IT IS!
YOU'RE JEALOUS THAT ALL THE CITIZENS OF GOTHAM CITY HAVE BECOME MY FANS!

JEALOUS? WHY WOULD I BE JEALOUS?

OH, SHUT UP!
IT'S OBVIOUS! UNTIL NOW, YOU WERE GOTHAM CITY'S HERO!

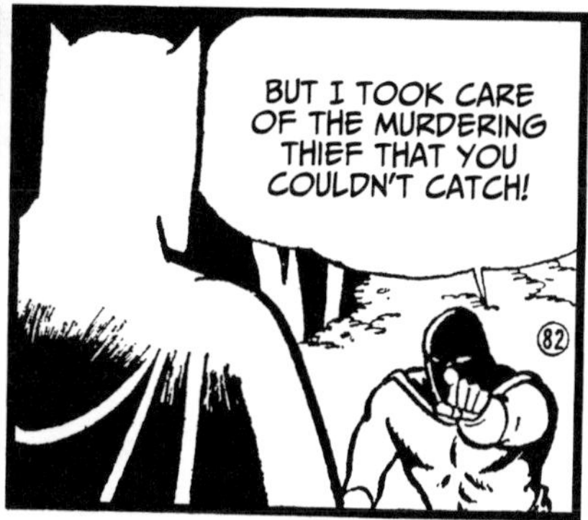
BUT I TOOK CARE OF THE MURDERING THIEF THAT YOU COULDN'T CATCH!

YOU'RE NOT THE HERO OF GOTHAM CITY ANYMORE!

THE HANGMAN IS!

IF YOU WANT TO TAKE MY HOOD OFF, GO AHEAD AND TRY!
COME ON!

HOLD IT! I'M NOT HERE TO FIGHT WITH YOU!

LOST YOUR NERVE? THEN I'LL UNMASK YOU AND SHOW EVERYBODY YOUR REAL STUPID FACE!

ARRRH!

HOLD ON, I SAID!

SFX: FWISH

SFX: HOIST

ENOUGH!

SFX: WHOK

NOW YOU DID IT. DO YOU REALLY THINK YOU CAN BEAT A PRO WRESTLER?!

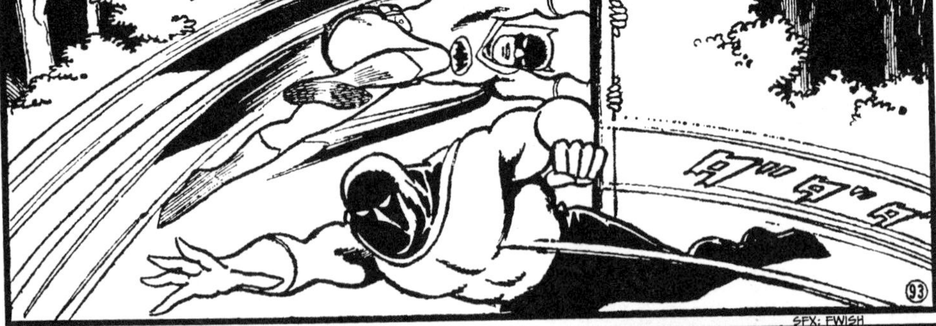

SFX: FWISH

SFX: WHIZZZ

SFX: WHOK
SFX: GRAB
NUTS! HE GOT A HOLD OF MY FEET!
SFX: FWOOSH
SFX: CRASH
SFX: WHUD

≈CHUCKLE≈ NOW DO YOU UNDERSTAND HOW STRONG A PRO WRESTLER IS?

SFX: KRAK

SFX: THUD

≈CHUCKLE≈ LOOKS LIKE YOU'RE DOWN FOR THE COUNT...

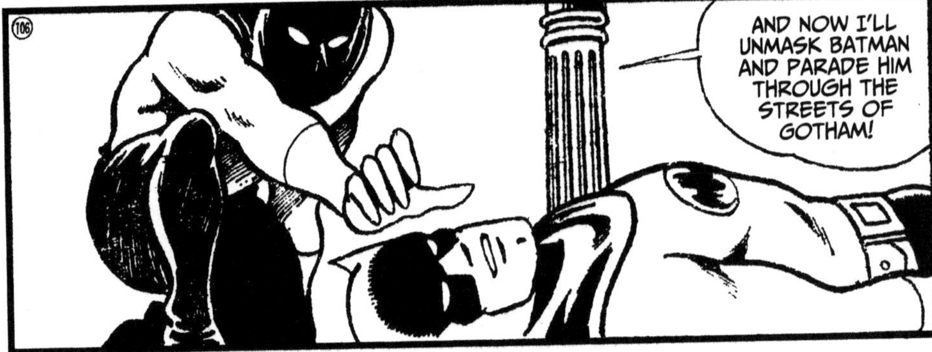

AND NOW I'LL UNMASK BATMAN AND PARADE HIM THROUGH THE STREETS OF GOTHAM!

ン家墓地

★ THE HANGMAN OF TERROR Part 3 ★

BATMAN EXCLUSIVE JAPANESE VERSION SHONEN GAHOSHA

Jiro Kuwata

I'M THIS CITY'S HERO NOW!
CHUCKLE YOU'RE GOTHAM CITY'S CHAMPION NO MORE!
1

LAST EPISODE...
Batman tried to get to the bottom of the mysterious activities of the masked wrestler The Hangman but ended up on the receiving end of the wrestler's finishing move. Then the wrestler reached out to remove Batman's mask...

I'M GOING TO TAKE OFF YOUR MASK AND LEARN YOUR IDENTITY.

ダ"ダ"ダ"ダ"
MM?

UH-OH! SOMEONE'S COMING...

SFX: VRRRRRRR

SFX: VRRR

BATMAN!
OHHHH...

I-I GOT BEAT UP BY THE HANGMAN...
HUH? BY THE HANGMAN?!

The two return to the Batcave...

IT SEEMS THE HANGMAN SEES ME AS HIS ADVERSARY...
I WONDER WHY...

BY THE WAY, ROBIN...
HAVE YOU FOUND THAT MYSTERY GIRL YET?

NOPE. I SPENT ALL DAY SEARCHING FOR HER IN GOTHAM CITY...

...BUT I'LL GET BACK OUT THERE TONIGHT TO CONTINUE THE HUNT.
GOOD. I HAVE A FEELING THAT IF WE CAN JUST FIND HER, WE'LL LEARN SOMETHING.

SFX: VRRRRRR
WHOA, WHAT'S THIS?
SFX: VRRRR

THAT GIRL, AND SHE INTENDS TO COMMIT SUICIDE?!

OH, NO! SHE JUMPED!

SFX: SPLOOSH

SFX: FWISH

SFX: SPLASH

WHERE'S THE GIRL? IT'S SO DARK DOWN HERE, I CAN BARELY SEE...

MMM... THERE!

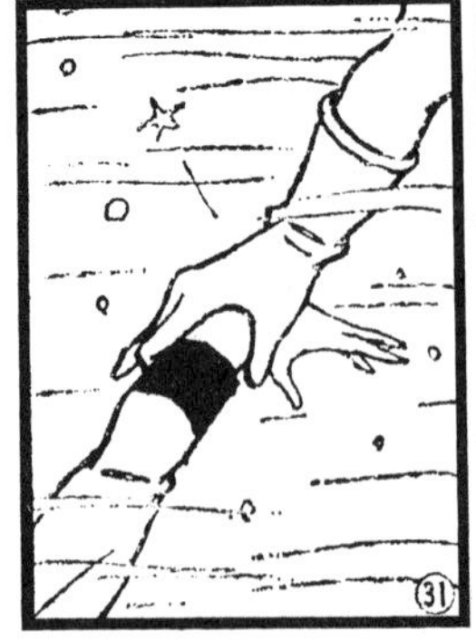

SHE'S UNCONSCIOUS. I'VE GOTTA GET HER TO A HOSPITAL!

病院

SIGN: HOSPITAL

SHE'LL BE ALL RIGHT. LUCKILY, SHE DIDN'T SWALLOW TOO MUCH WATER.
I'M SURE SHE'LL RECOVER QUICKLY.

GOOD. I'LL CALL BATMAN RIGHT AWAY.

SFX: RING RING RING RING

HI, ROBIN. DID YOU FIND THE GIRL?

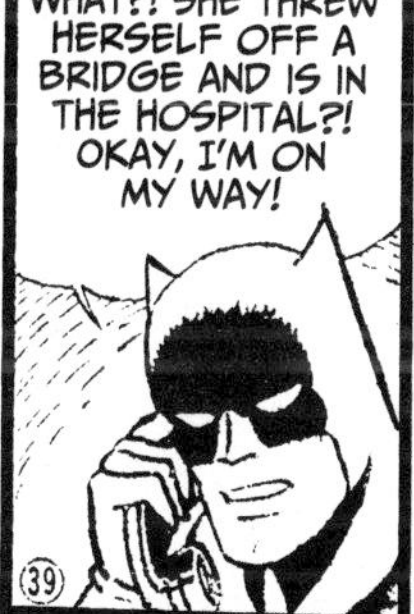
WHAT?! SHE THREW HERSELF OFF A BRIDGE AND IS IN THE HOSPITAL?! OKAY, I'M ON MY WAY!

NOW WE JUST HAVE TO WAIT FOR HER TO WAKE UP. WE HAVE LOTS OF QUESTIONS FOR HER AND I HAVE A FEELING SHE'S GOT THE ANSWERS...

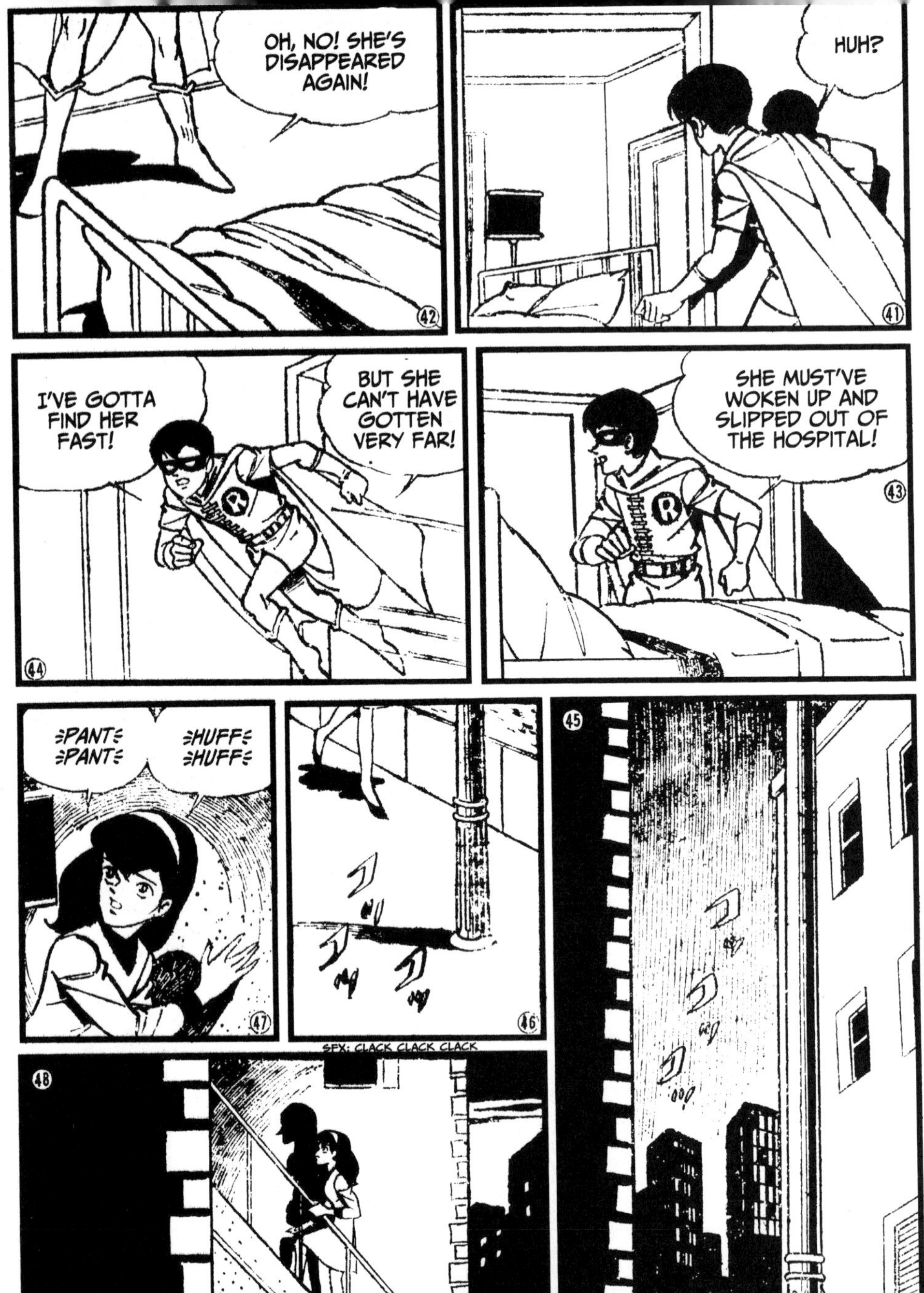
HUH?
OH, NO! SHE'S DISAPPEARED AGAIN!
SHE MUST'VE WOKEN UP AND SLIPPED OUT OF THE HOSPITAL!
BUT SHE CAN'T HAVE GOTTEN VERY FAR!
I'VE GOTTA FIND HER FAST!
HUFF HUFF
PANT PANT
SFX: CLACK CLACK CLACK
SFX: CLACK CLACK CLACK

SFX: SLUMP

SOB SOB

I THOUGHT IF I DIED, MY BROTHER WOULD COME TO HIS SENSES...

...BUT I GUESS GOD DOESN'T WANT ME TO DIE YET.

WHY DOES A GIRL LIKE YOU WANT TO DIE ANYWAY?

SFX: SWISH

WOULD YOU EXPLAIN THAT TO ME?

ROBIN!

WHEN DID YOU...?
I FOLLOWED YOU HERE.

I CAN SEE YOU HAVE A REASON FOR ATTEMPTING SUICIDE. TELL ME WHAT IT IS.

...

WELL?
I-I CAN'T...
DON'T ASK ME THAT!
THEN WHAT'S YOUR NAME?
IT'S CATHY.
I CAN'T TELL YOU ANYTHING MORE THAN THAT.
WHY NOT? WHAT KIND OF SECRET ARE YOU KEEPING?
WHAT KIND OF CRIME WAS YOUR BROTHER GOING TO COMMIT THAT NIGHT?
AND WHO IS YOUR BROTHER?!
I CAN'T! I CAN'T! I CAN'T TELL YOU!
ギイーッ
SFX: CREAK
AH!

BROTHER...

BROTHER? THIS BIG GUY IS YOUR BROTHER, CATHY?

CATHY! WHAT DID YOU TELL THIS BRAT?!

I-I DIDN'T TELL HIM ANYTHING! REALLY!

ROBIN, PLEASE! GET OUT OF HERE NOW! OTHERWISE MY BROTHER WILL KILL YOU!
KILL ME?

SORRY. I CAN'T AFFORD TO LET YOU GO HOME.

WHAT ARE YOU DOING?!

SFX: FWISH

BROTHER, DON'T! ROBIN DOESN'T KNOW ANYTHING!

SFX: KRAK

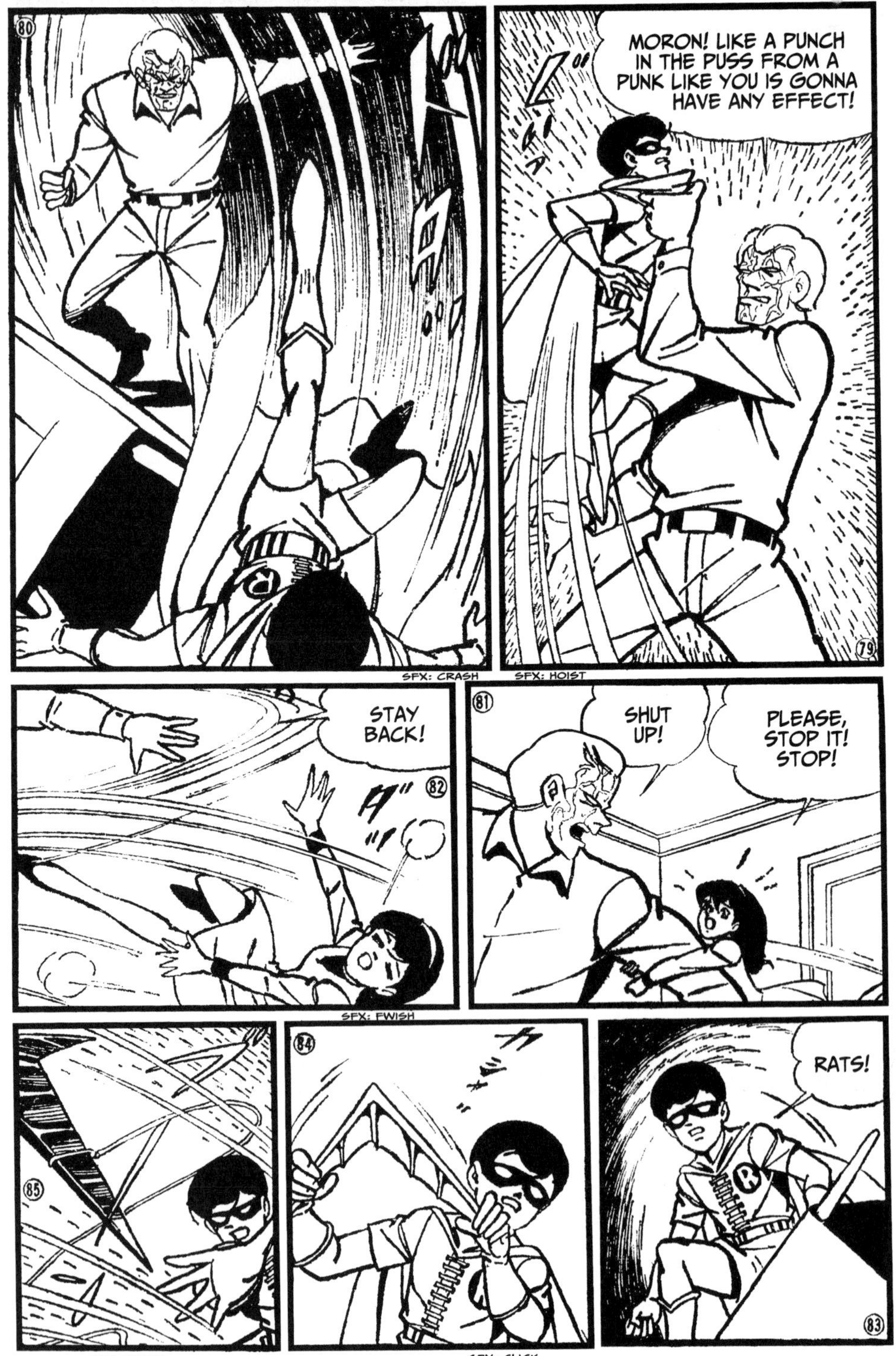
MORON! LIKE A PUNCH IN THE PUSS FROM A PUNK LIKE YOU IS GONNA HAVE ANY EFFECT!
SFX: HOIST
SFX: CRASH
PLEASE, STOP IT! STOP!
SHUT UP!
STAY BACK!
SFX: FWISH
RATS!
SFX: CLICK
SFX: SWISH

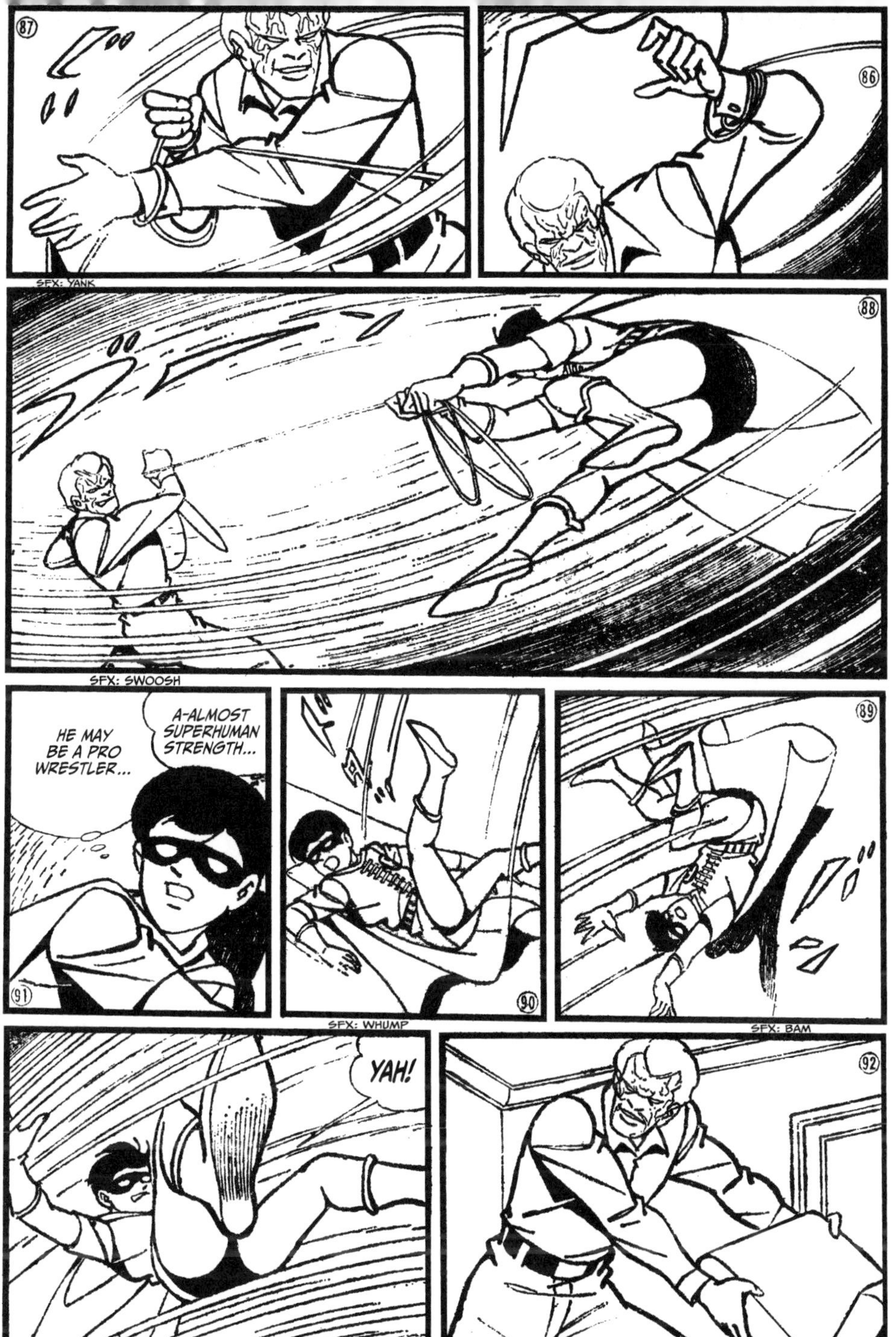
SFX: YANK
SFX: SWOOSH
SFX: BAM
SFX: WHUMP
A-ALMOST SUPERHUMAN STRENGTH...
HE MAY BE A PRO WRESTLER...
YAH!

SFX: KRAK

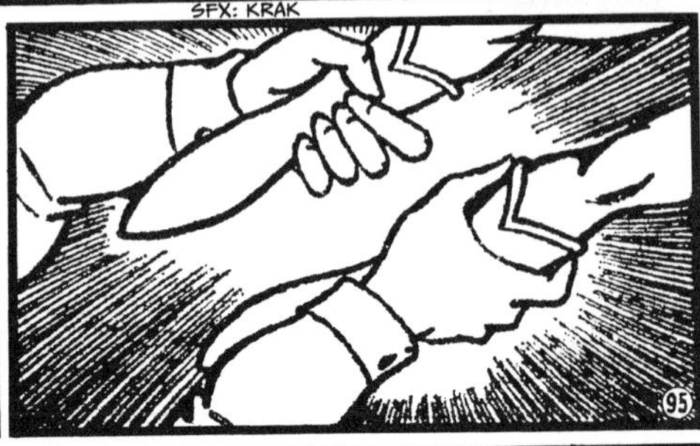

ARRHH!

SFX: CRASH

ALL THE FIGHT'S OUT OF YOU, EH, BRAT? ≈CHUCKLE≈

HUH? WHERE'S CATHY?
CATHY! CATHY! WHERE'D YOU GO?!
DAMMIT! DID SHE RUN OFF SOMEWHERE?
I DON'T THINK SHE'D TURN HER OWN BROTHER IN TO THE POLICE...
...BUT ANYWAY, I GOTTA GET RID OF THIS KID. THAT'S THE ONLY WAY I'LL HAVE ANY PEACE OF MIND.
SFX: VROOOO

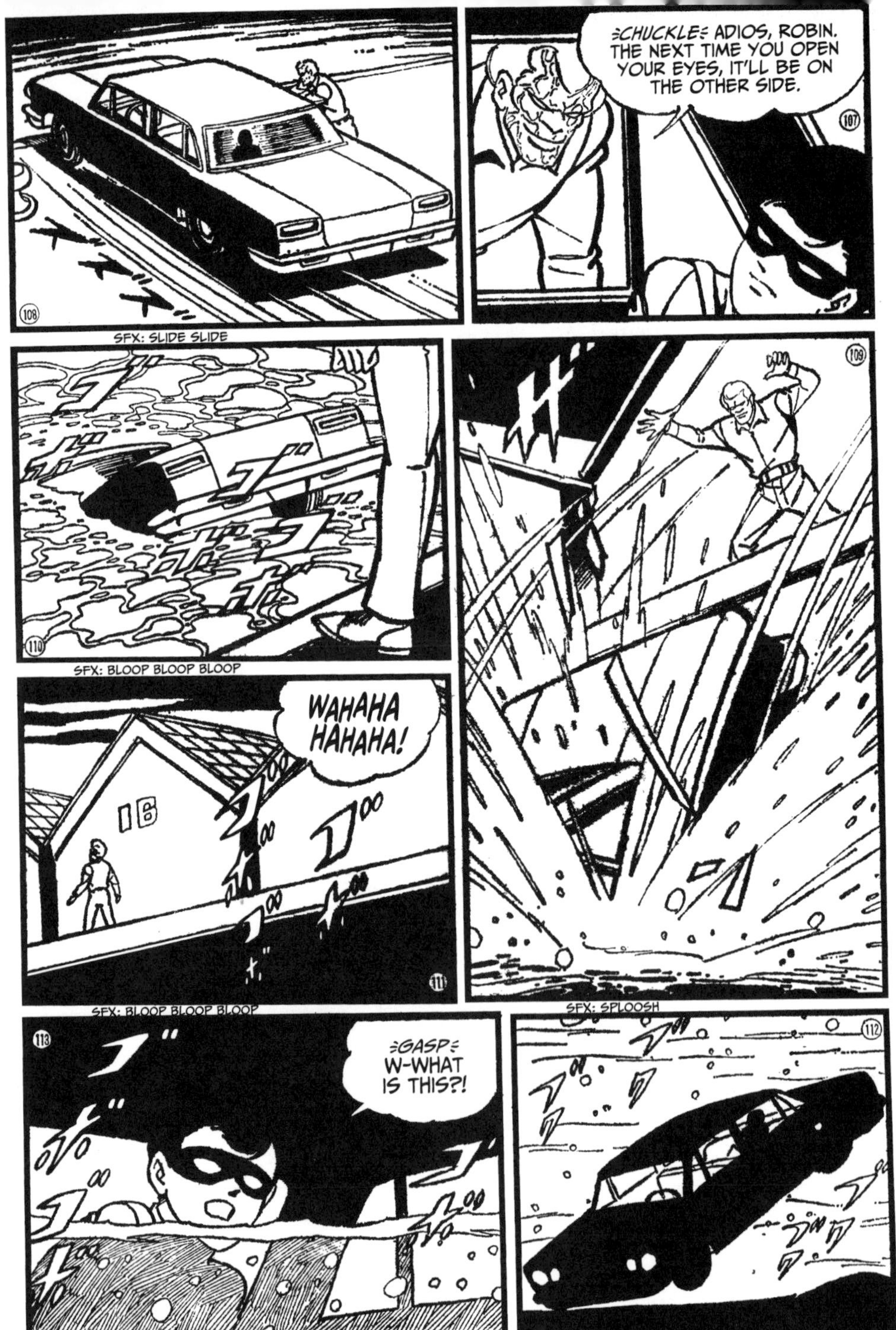

=CHUCKLE= ADIOS, ROBIN. THE NEXT TIME YOU OPEN YOUR EYES, IT'LL BE ON THE OTHER SIDE.
SFX: SLIDE SLIDE
SFX: SPLOOSH
SFX: BLOOP BLOOP BLOOP
WAHAHA HAHAHA!
SFX: BLOOP BLOOP BLOOP
SFX: BLUB BLUB BLUB BLUB
=GASP= W-WHAT IS THIS?!
SFX: BLOOP BLOOP BLOOP

バットマン
★THE HANGMAN OF TERROR Part 4★
BATMAN
EXCLUSIVE
JAPANESE VERSION
SHONEN GAHOSHA
© N.P.P. 1966
Jiro Kuwata

LAST EPISODE...
Robin found the mystery girl at last and her name is Cathy, but that's all the information he could get out of her. Then Cathy's strapping big brother entered and attacked Robin. The brutish brother knocked out the Boy Wonder, tied him up, and sank him into the sea inside of a car...

SFX: BLOOP BLOOP BLOOP

GASP

I'M IN A CAR...
...AND TIED UP!

SFX: BLOOP BLOOP

T-THEN THAT BIG GUY MUST'VE PLUNGED THIS CAR AND ME INTO THE SEA WHILE I WAS OUT COLD!

THAT RAT! I CAN'T EVEN OPEN THE DOOR WITH MY HANDS TIED...

NO GOOD... THE INSIDE OF THE CAR'S FILLING UP WITH WATER!

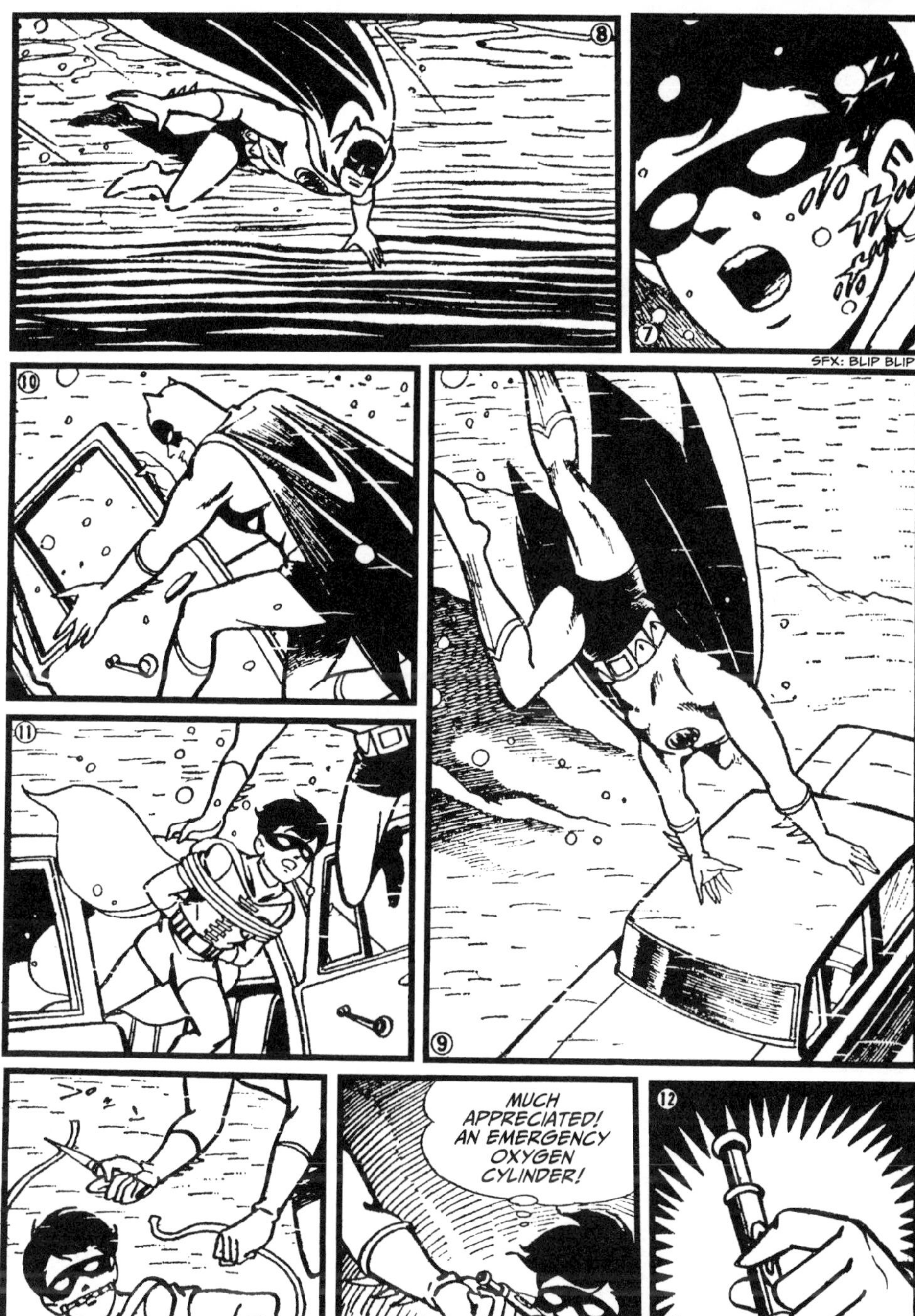
SFX: BLIP BLIP
MUCH APPRECIATED! AN EMERGENCY OXYGEN CYLINDER!

CLOSE CALL! IF I'D BEEN A MINUTE OR TWO LATE, IT WOULD'VE BEEN TOO LATE FOR YOU, CHUM!

PHEW...
BATMAN! HOW DID YOU KNOW I WAS HERE?!

THE GIRL, I THINK SHE SAID HER NAME WAS CATHY...
SHE CALLED THE HOSPITAL.

IT'S A SHAME. I FOUND HER, ONLY TO LOSE HER AGAIN. AND IT'S A SAFE BET NEITHER ONE OF THEM WILL BE GOING BACK TO THAT APARTMENT.

BATMAN, DO YOU THINK CATHY'S BROTHER COULD BE THE HANGMAN?
HMM... WHAT DOES HE LOOK LIKE?

HE'S A BIG GUY WITH SCARS ALL OVER HIS FACE...

HMM... SCARS, EH?

ゴッタム警察署

SIGN: GOTHAM POLICE STATION

WHAT?
YOU WANT TO KNOW IF THERE'S ANY RECORD OF A PRO WRESTLER WHO DIED IN A FIRE?

HOLD ON. WE'LL SOON FIND OUT.

CHIEF GORDON! THERE'S NO FIRE INVOLVED, BUT THIS MAY BE SOMETHING!
THEN GIVE IT HERE!

HMM... ULTRAGUN! AN UP-AND-COMING PRO WRESTLER WHO MANY EXPECTED TO BECOME THE UNDEFEATED CHAMPION.

ABOUT THREE YEARS AGO, A PLANE CRASHED DURING TAKEOFF. SUPPOSEDLY, THIS WRESTLER WAS ON BOARD, BUT THEY DIDN'T FIND HIS BODY.

CAN I BORROW THIS PHOTO?
SURE, BUT WHAT DO YOU INTEND TO DO?

I HAVE AN IDEA.

COME ON, ROBIN. THE HANGMAN HAS ANOTHER MATCH TONIGHT.

体 育 館
SIGN: SPORTS ARENA

SFX: WAAA WAAA WAAA

AAAH!

SFX: WHUMP

≈CHUCKLE≈

1!
2!
3!

SFX: SWISH

ATTABOY!
THE BEST IN THE WORLD!
THE HANGMAN!

HOLD ON THERE, HANGMAN.
WELL, HI, BATMAN.

I CHALLENGE YOU TO A MATCH HERE AND NOW!

WHAT?
YOU CHALLENGE ME?

BUT IF I WIN, I'M TAKING THAT HOOD OFF!

≶CHUCKLE≶... YOU'RE ON! BUT IF I WIN, I'M RIPPIN' OFF *YOUR* MASK!

THEN WE HAVE A DEAL!

SFX: FWISH

WOW! A SHOWDOWN BETWEEN THE TWO CHAMPIONS OF GOTHAM CITY!

ALTHOUGH I DOUBT EVEN BATMAN CAN BEAT A PRO WRESTLER IN HIS NATURAL ELEMENT...

SFX: SWISH

SFX: KRAK

SFX: FWISH

SFX: WHAK

SFX: GRAB

SFX: WHOOSH
SFX: WHAM
SFX: SWISH
よろ よろ
SFX: STAGGER
SFX: GRAB
UH-OH! BATMAN'S FALLEN PREY TO THE HANGMAN'S SIGNATURE MOVE!

SFX: WHUMP

IT'S OVER!
THE HANGMAN DEFEATED BATMAN!

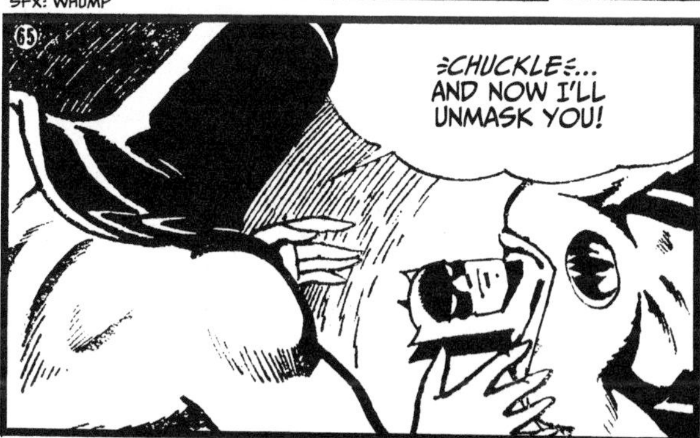
⁼CHUCKLE⁼... AND NOW I'LL UNMASK YOU!

WHA...?! THAT'S MY FACE!

NOW!
SFX: KRAK
SFX: WOK
SFX: WHUD
SFX: TUG

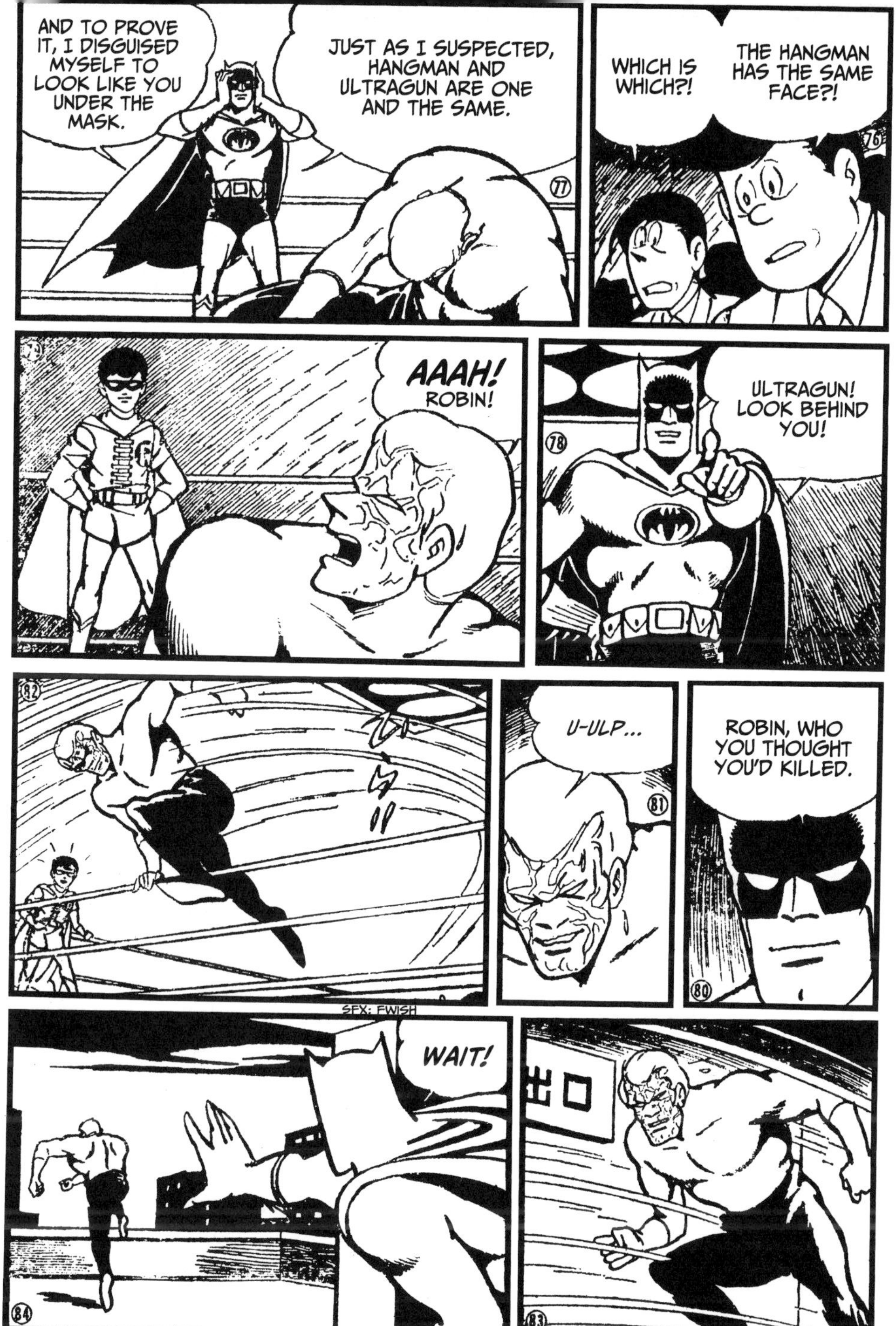

THE HANGMAN HAS THE SAME FACE?!
WHICH IS WHICH?!

JUST AS I SUSPECTED, HANGMAN AND ULTRAGUN ARE ONE AND THE SAME.
AND TO PROVE IT, I DISGUISED MYSELF TO LOOK LIKE YOU UNDER THE MASK.

ULTRAGUN! LOOK BEHIND YOU!

AAAH! ROBIN!

ROBIN, WHO YOU THOUGHT YOU'D KILLED.

U-ULP...

SFX: FWISH

WAIT!
SIGN: EXIT

SFX: SPIN

IT SEEMS YOU WIN, BATMAN.
OKAY, I'LL TELL YOU EVERYTHING YOU WANNA KNOW.

I WAS ONCE AN UNDEFEATED WRESTLER PEGGED TO BE THE FUTURE WORLD CHAMPION.

BUT AFTER MY FACE WAS MESSED UP IN THAT PLANE ACCIDENT, I TOOK TO WEARIN' A HOOD.
I CALLED MYSELF THE HANGMAN AND TORE UP THE RING.

I THOUGHT I COULD BE A HERO, BUT THE MORE MATCHES I WON, THE MORE THE CROWDS HATED ME.

I WAS DEVASTATED, BATMAN! I WANTED THE CITIZENS OF GOTHAM CITY TO RESPECT ME AS A HERO LIKE THEY DO YOU!

SO I TRICKED FORMER PRO WRESTLER TIGER KID, WHO HAD MUSH FOR BRAINS. I HAD HIM ROB THAT JEWELRY STORE WHILE DRESSED UP LIKE ME AND WHEN HE ESCAPED TO THE ROOF LIKE I TOLD HIM TO, I AMBUSHED THE POOR SAP AND THREW HIM TO HIS DEATH.

PEOPLE WHO DIDN'T KNOW SQUAT HAILED ME AS A HERO FOR TAKIN' OUT A ROBBER.

BUT I GUESS I COULDN'T FOOL YOU TWO...

MY PLAN WAS TO EVENTUALLY OUTWIT YOU AND BECOME GOTHAM CITY'S HERO IN YOUR PLACE...

...BUT IT JUST DIDN'T WORK OUT.
EXACTLY. YOU CAN'T FOOL ALL THE PEOPLE ALL THE TIME.

YA GOT THAT RIGHT, BATMAN.
NOW COME ON. LET'S GO TO THE POLICE.

NOTHIN' DOING! FOR WHAT I DID, I'LL PUNCH MY OWN TICKET!
SFX: SWISH

AH!
HE JUMPED!

...

BROTHER!

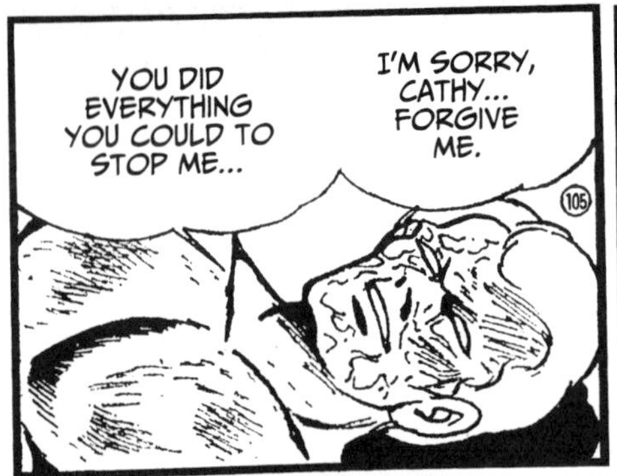
I'M SORRY, CATHY... FORGIVE ME.
YOU DID EVERYTHING YOU COULD TO STOP ME...

BROTHER!

SFX: THUD

BROTHER! BROTHER!

SFX: WHEEE-OOO WHEEE-OOO

バットマン
★ FIEND OF THE MASQUERADE FESTIVAL ★
BATMAN
EXCLUSIVE
JAPANESE VERSION
SHONEN GAHOSHA
© N.P.P. 1966
Jiro Kuwata

SFX: VROOO

SFX: VROOO

THAT'S THE STATE PENITENTIARY WHERE KELSON IS LOCKED UP.

SFX: SKREEE

SFX: CLACK CLACK CLACK CLACK

WELL, HELLO THERE, BATMAN AND ROBIN!
I'VE BEEN WAITING FOR YOU.

WE CAME AS SOON AS WE HEARD THE NEWS THAT KELSON HAD ESCAPED, WARDEN.

YES, TERRIBLE THING. KELSON WAS IN HERE FOR DEALING IN STOLEN JEWELS...

...BUT IT SEEMS HE HAD OUTSIDE HELP ESCAPING.
I SEE...
BUT WHO WOULD DO THAT?

IF YOU FIND THE ANSWER TO THAT, YOU'LL BE ABLE TO CATCH KELSON...

WARDEN, COULD I SPEAK WITH KELSON'S CELLMATE?
CERTAINLY.

BRING OVER THE PRISONER FROM CELL NUMBER NINE.

THIS IS KELSON'S CELLMATE.
HEH-HEH-HEH...

DO YOU REMEMBER WHAT YOU AND KELSON TALKED ABOUT BEFORE HIS ESCAPE?
NOW THAT YOU MENTION IT...

...KELSON WAS ALWAYS BRAGGING ABOUT...
...THIS FRIEND HE HAD WHO WOULD GIVE HIM A LOT OF MONEY AND MOVE HIM TO ANOTHER COUNTRY WHEN HE GOT OUTTA HERE.

AND WHO IS THIS FRIEND?

BEATS ME.
ONLY...

...HE SAID THEY WERE GONNA MEET UP AT A FESTIVAL IN GOTHAM CITY.

A FESTIVAL...
BATMAN! IT HAS TO BE THE MASQUERADE FESTIVAL!

HMM... BUT IT'S CUSTOMARY FOR PARTICIPANTS OF THAT FESTIVAL TO WEAR A MASK.
SO YOU DON'T KNOW WHO IS WHO...

FINDING KELSON IN A CROWD LIKE THAT...
...WOULD BE LIKE SEARCHING FOR A NEEDLE IN A HAYSTACK.

ANYWAY, LET'S GO TO THE MASQUERADE FEST.

SFX: VROOO

SFX: POP POP

仮装まつり

SIGN: MASQUERADE FESTIVAL

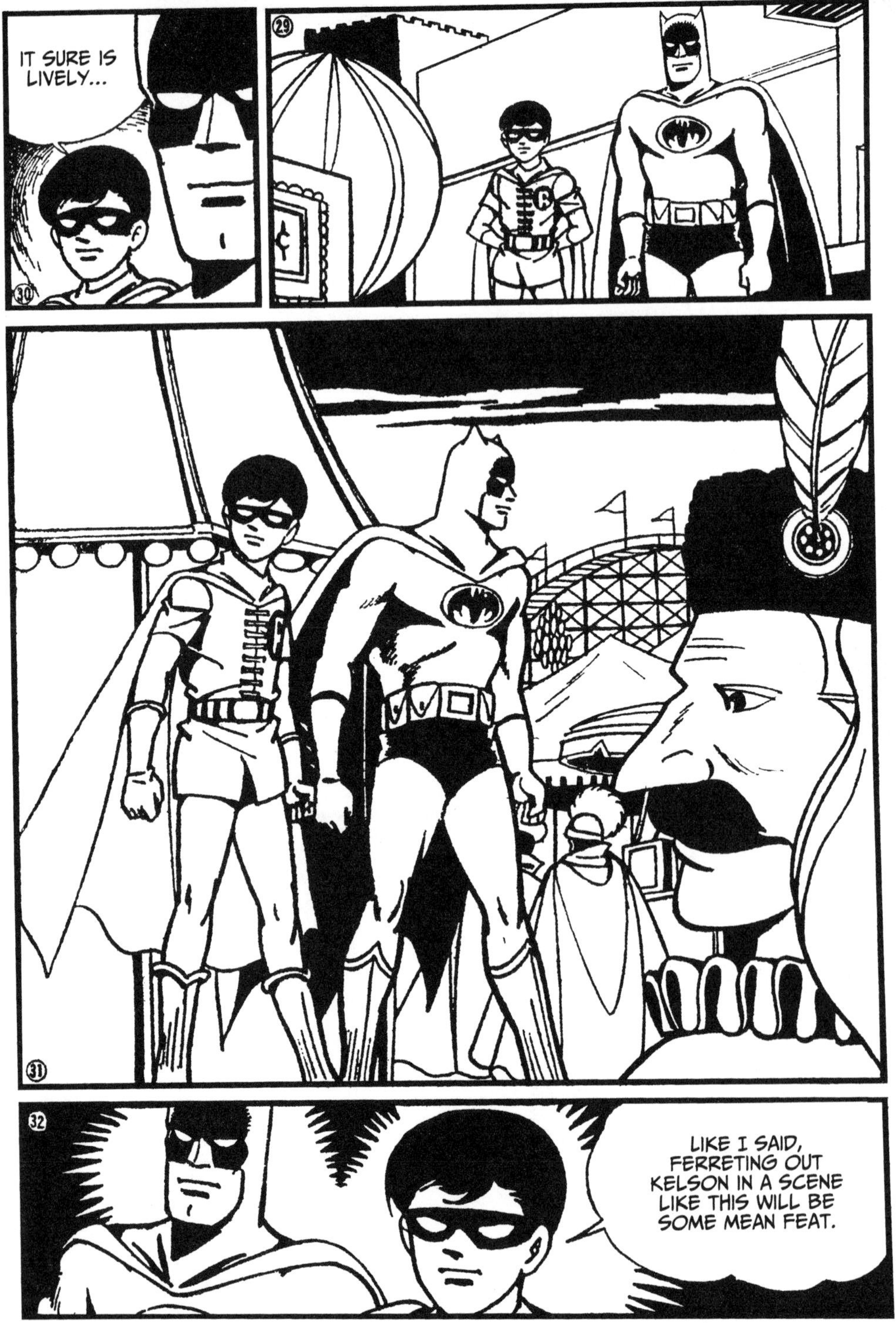

IT SURE IS LIVELY...

LIKE I SAID, FERRETING OUT KELSON IN A SCENE LIKE THIS WILL BE SOME MEAN FEAT.

LET'S START BY PAYING A VISIT TO THE SPONSOR OF THE FESTIVAL.

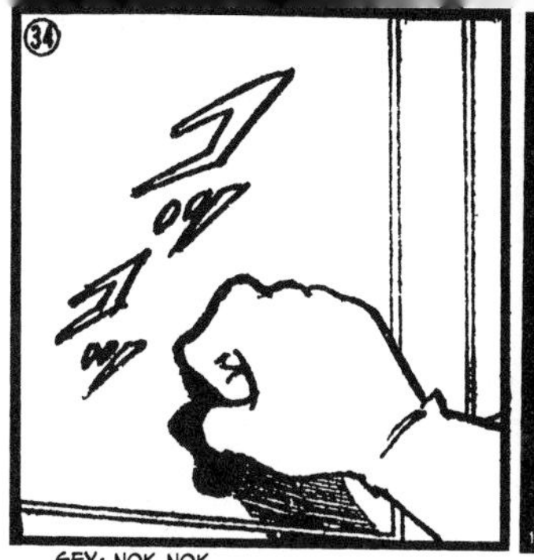
SFX: NOK NOK

WELL, WELL, WHAT A PLEASANT SURPRISE. BATMAN AND ROBIN! WELCOME.

I'M ASHLEY, THE HOST OF THIS FESTIVAL.
PLEASURE TO MEET YOU.

BUT I SUSPECT YOU'RE NOT JUST HERE FOR A SOCIAL CALL?
ACTUALLY...

...AN ESCAPED PRISONER HAS MELTED INTO THE CROWD HERE.

ESCAPED PRISONER?!

WE'RE HERE TO CATCH HIM, BUT I'D LIKE YOUR COOPERATION.
CERTAINLY. I'D BE HAPPY TO HELP.

I'VE BEEN CRISSCROSSING THE U.S. WITH MY MASQUERADE FESTIVAL AND THIS TIME, I WANT IT TO BE AN UNQUALIFIED SUCCESS.

?
CHUCKLE
AN ESCAPED CONVICT, HUH?

IF A CRIMINAL SLIPS INTO THE CROWD AT THIS FESTIVAL...
...I THINK YOU'RE OUTTA LUCK, PAL.

WHO'S THIS?

OH, THIS IS BURTON, ONE OF MY SECURITY OFFICERS.

AS YOU KNOW, EVERYBODY HERE IS WEARING A MASK...
...SO WHO KNOWS WHO'S WHO?

BUT THAT BEING SAID, I'LL DO WHATEVER I CAN TO HELP YOU, BATMAN.

MY OTHER SECURITY OFFICER IS TOM DAWES...

...BUT UNFORTUNATELY, HE SEEMS TO BE PATROLLING THE GROUNDS AT THE MOMENT.

I THINK WE'LL STROLL AROUND AS WELL.

HUH? IT'S BATMAN!
OH, COME ON! IT'S JUST SOMEBODY IN DISGUISE.

SOUNDS LIKE PEOPLE THINK WE'RE PART OF THE MASQUERADE...
THAT'LL MAKE IT EASIER FOR US TO DO OUR JOB.

WELL, WELL! MY EYES DON'T DECEIVE ME. YOU'RE THE REAL BATMAN AND ROBIN!

PHOTOGRAPHER VICKI VALE! HI!

LONG TIME NO SEE.
I'M HERE TO TAKE PHOTOS FOR WORK.

AH! WHAT'S THAT?

SFX: WHUMP

A MAN FELL OFF THE MERRY-GO-ROUND!

HUH? THIS MAN IS...

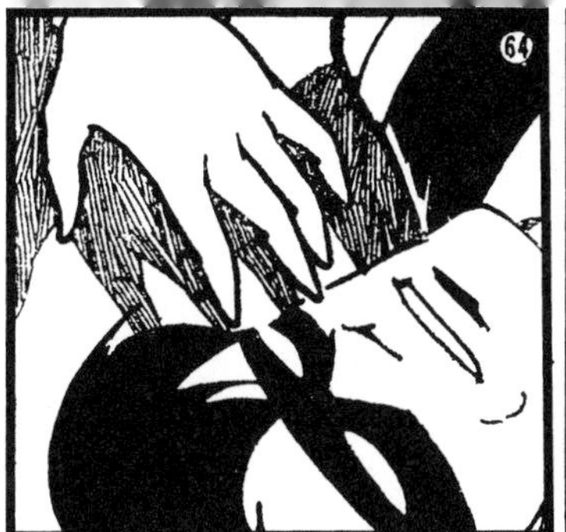

IT IS HIM!
THE ESCAPEE, KELSON!

JEEPERS, WHAT A WAY TO GO!

YOU THINK IT'S A HEART ATTACK?
NO. LOOK CLOSELY AT KELSON'S NECK.

WHAT IS IT?
A POISONED NEEDLE!

THEN KELSON WAS MURDERED...
THAT'S RIGHT. THERE'S A KILLER HERE!

ROBIN, SCAN THE CROWD. SEE IF ANYONE SUSPICIOUS STANDS OUT.

MM?

YOU OVER THERE!
STAY WHERE YOU ARE!

SFX: TWITCH

SFX: FWISH

TRYING TO GET AWAY, *EH?*

AAAH!

OH, NO! OH, NO! OH, NO!

I NEED TO BORROW THIS!
SFX: SWISH
H-HELP!
SFX: FWISH
SFX: BOING

AAAAH!

SFX: CRASH

SFX: KRAK

HUFF HUFF...

ARGH!
SFX: BAM

PLEASE CHECK THIS GUY OUT, BATMAN.

SFX: WHUMP

WAAAAH! WAAAH!
MOMMY! SOB

THEY'RE BULLYING ME!
WHAT'S THIS GUY'S PROBLEM?

TAKE OFF THAT MASK!

I DIDN'T DO ANYTHING!
SOB SOB

WHY, IT'S "WEEPING" WILLOW, THE PETTY THIEF!

WHY DID YOU RUN AWAY AFTER KELSON WAS MURDERED?
WAAAH!
A-AFTER ALL, KELSON AND I DIDN'T GET ALONG.

SO I FIGURED I'D BE SUSPECTED...
WAAAH! WAAAH!

I DIDN'T KILL THE GUY! HELP ME!
WAAAAH!

CERTAINLY, WILLOW ISN'T THE MURDEROUS TYPE...
SOMEONE ELSE MUST HAVE DONE IT.

WHO ARE YOU?

I'M TOM DAWES, A SECURITY OFFICER HERE.
BURTON IS MY PARTNER.

I HURT MY LEG, SO I'M STILL HOBBLING AROUND ON THIS.

ANYWAY, ASSUMING "WEEPING" WILLOW ISN'T OUR KILLER, THERE MUST BE SOME CLUE...

I'VE GOT A CLUE.

VICKI! WHAT IS IT?

I HAPPENED TO TAKE A PHOTO RIGHT BEFORE THAT MAN WAS MURDERED.

THIS IS IT!

THIS MAN IS KELSON...

...BUT THE OTHER ONE IS DISGUISED AS A MUSKETEER.

AND KELSON IS HANDING THE MUSKETEER A PACKAGE OF SOME SORT.

MY GUT TELLS ME THIS MUSKETEER AIDED IN KELSON'S PRISON BREAK.
AND THAT HE ALSO MURDERED KELSON!

COME ON, ROBIN! LET'S LOOK FOR THE MUSKETEER.
I'M SURE HE DOESN'T KNOW HE WAS CAUGHT ON FILM.

IF YOU SEE HIM, SEND ME A SIGNAL WITH YOUR BELT TRANSMITTER.
OKAY!

MM?
SFX: BEEP BEEP
BATMAN! I SPOTTED THE MUSKETEER AND AM TAILING HIM NOW.
GOOD WORK! I'LL BE RIGHT THERE.
SFX: SWISH
SFX: FWISH

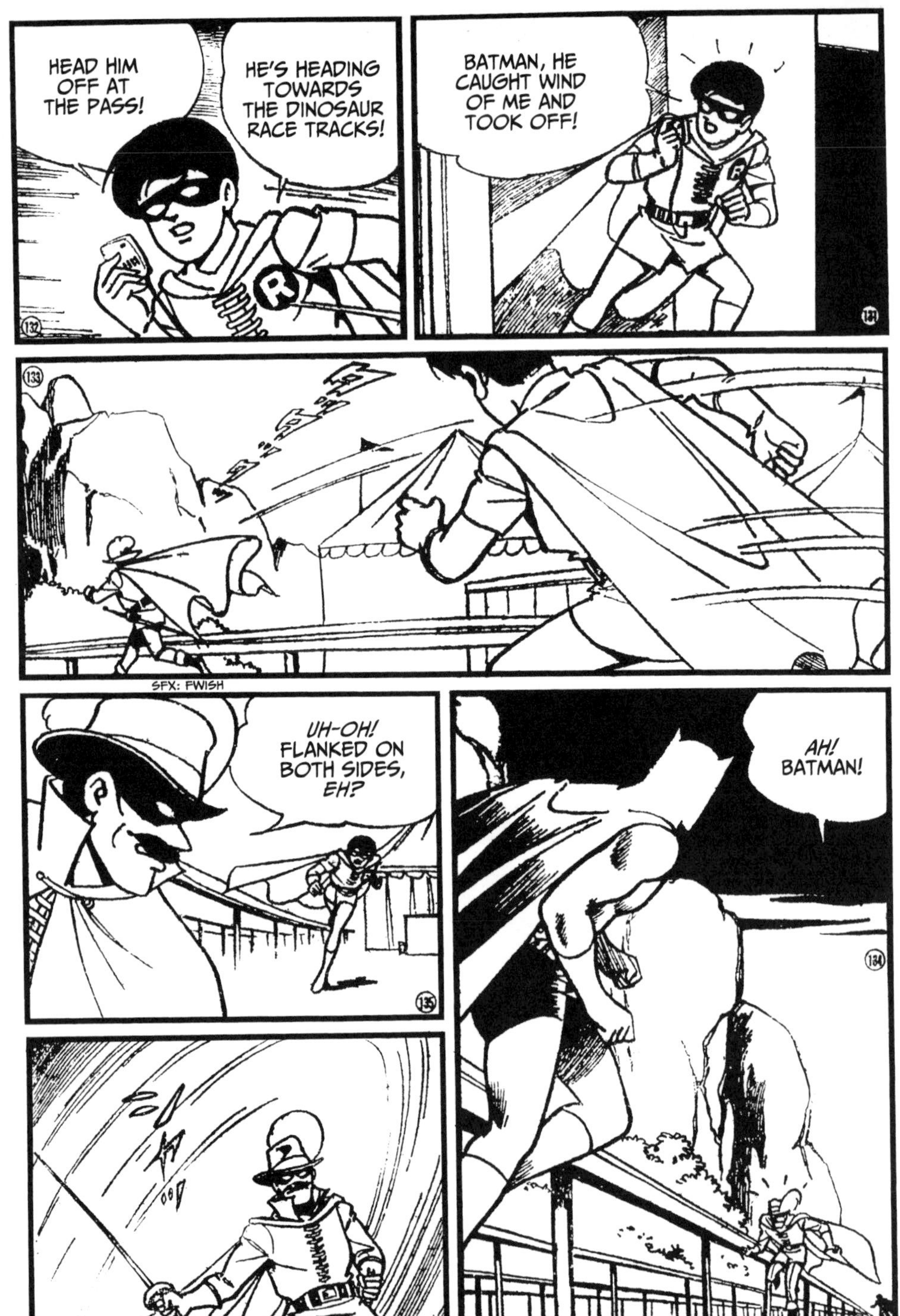

BATMAN, HE CAUGHT WIND OF ME AND TOOK OFF!
HE'S HEADING TOWARDS THE DINOSAUR RACE TRACKS!
HEAD HIM OFF AT THE PASS!
SFX: FWISH
AH! BATMAN!
UH-OH! FLANKED ON BOTH SIDES, EH?
SFX: SWISH

SFX: WHIZZ

GASP

SFX: TAK TAK

SON OF A GUN! HE MEANS TO GET AWAY BY CUTTING ACROSS THE TRACKS!

AFTER HIM, ROBIN! HE MUST BE THE KILLER!

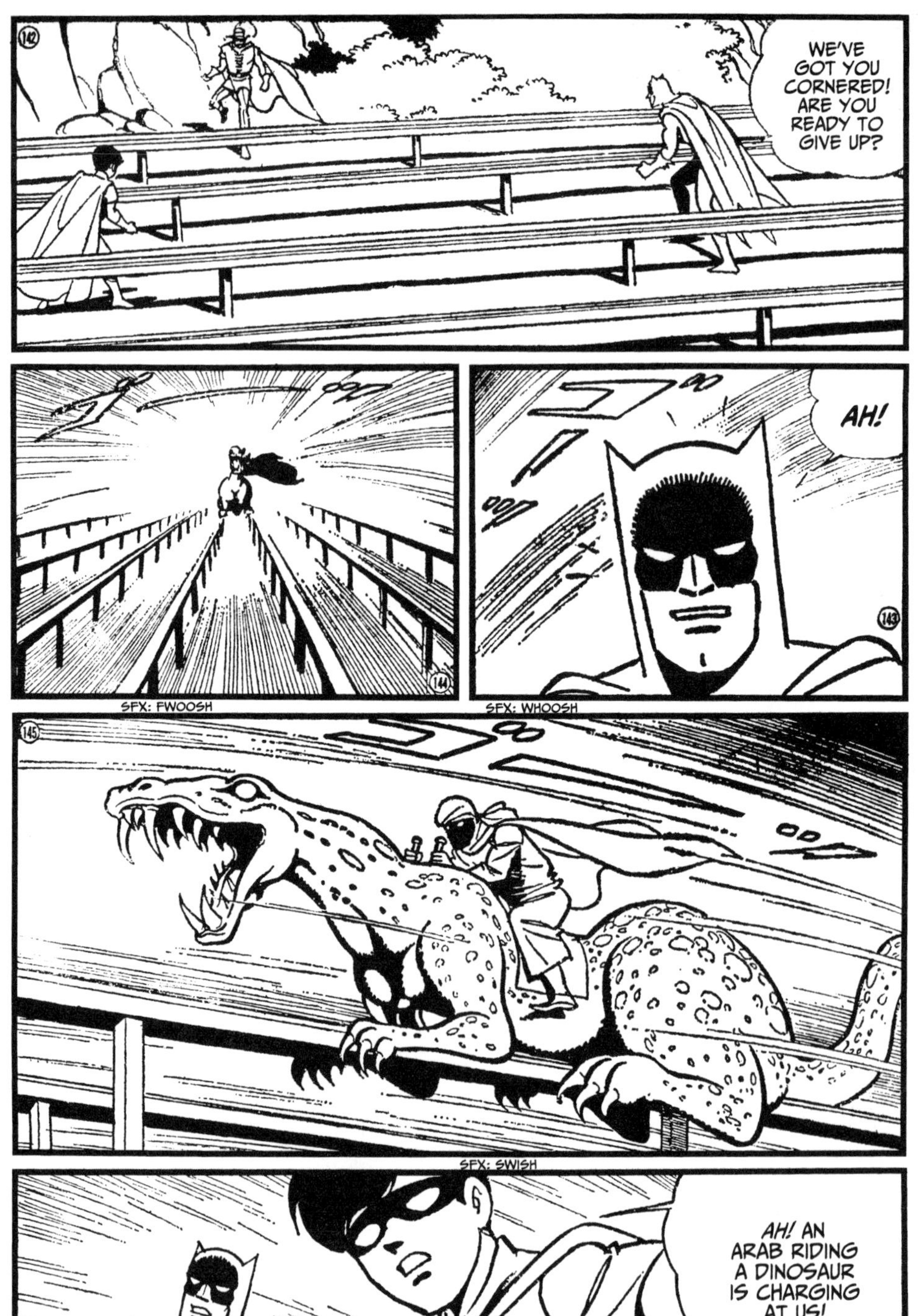
142
WE'VE GOT YOU CORNERED! ARE YOU READY TO GIVE UP?
143
AH!
144
SFX: FWOOSH
SFX: WHOOSH
145
SFX: SWISH
146
AH! AN ARAB RIDING A DINOSAUR IS CHARGING AT US!

SFX: FWOOSH

ROBIN, DUCK!

SFX: FWISH

SFX: WHOOSH

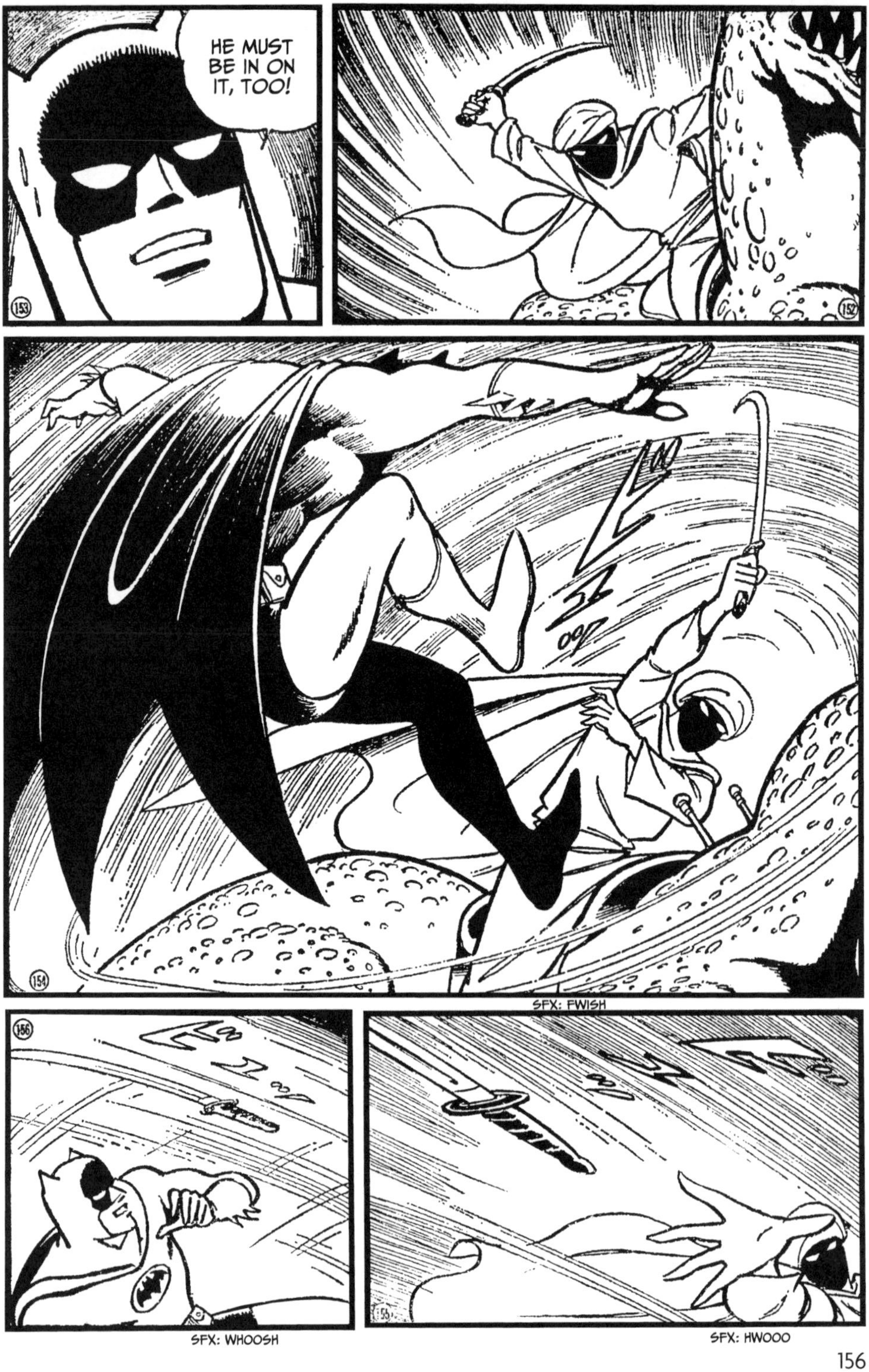

HE MUST BE IN ON IT, TOO!

SFX: FWISH

SFX: HWOOO

SFX: WHOOSH

HEY! HELP!

SFX: SWISH

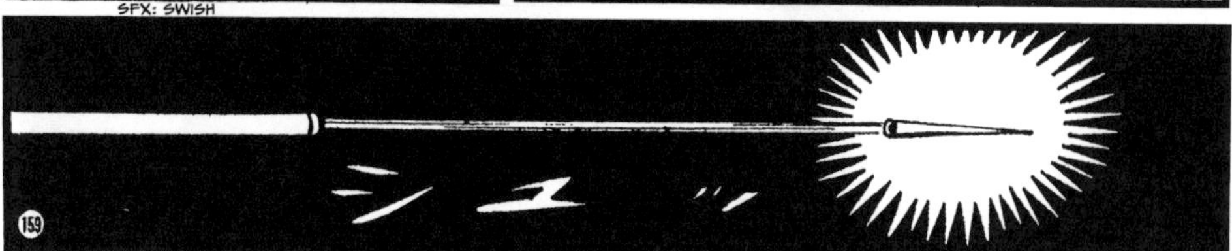
SFX: FSSHH

UNGH!

SFX: TUMBLE

SFX: WHUMP

AH! THE ARAB SHOT THE MUSKETEER!

SFX: WHOOSH

H-HE'S DEAD?!

WHO IS THIS MUSKETEER?

WHAT THE...?! IT'S BURTON, THE FIRST SECURITY OFFICER WE MET!

AND LOOK! THIS POISON-TIPPED DART IN HIS THROAT IS THE SAME KIND THAT WAS USED TO KILL KELSON!

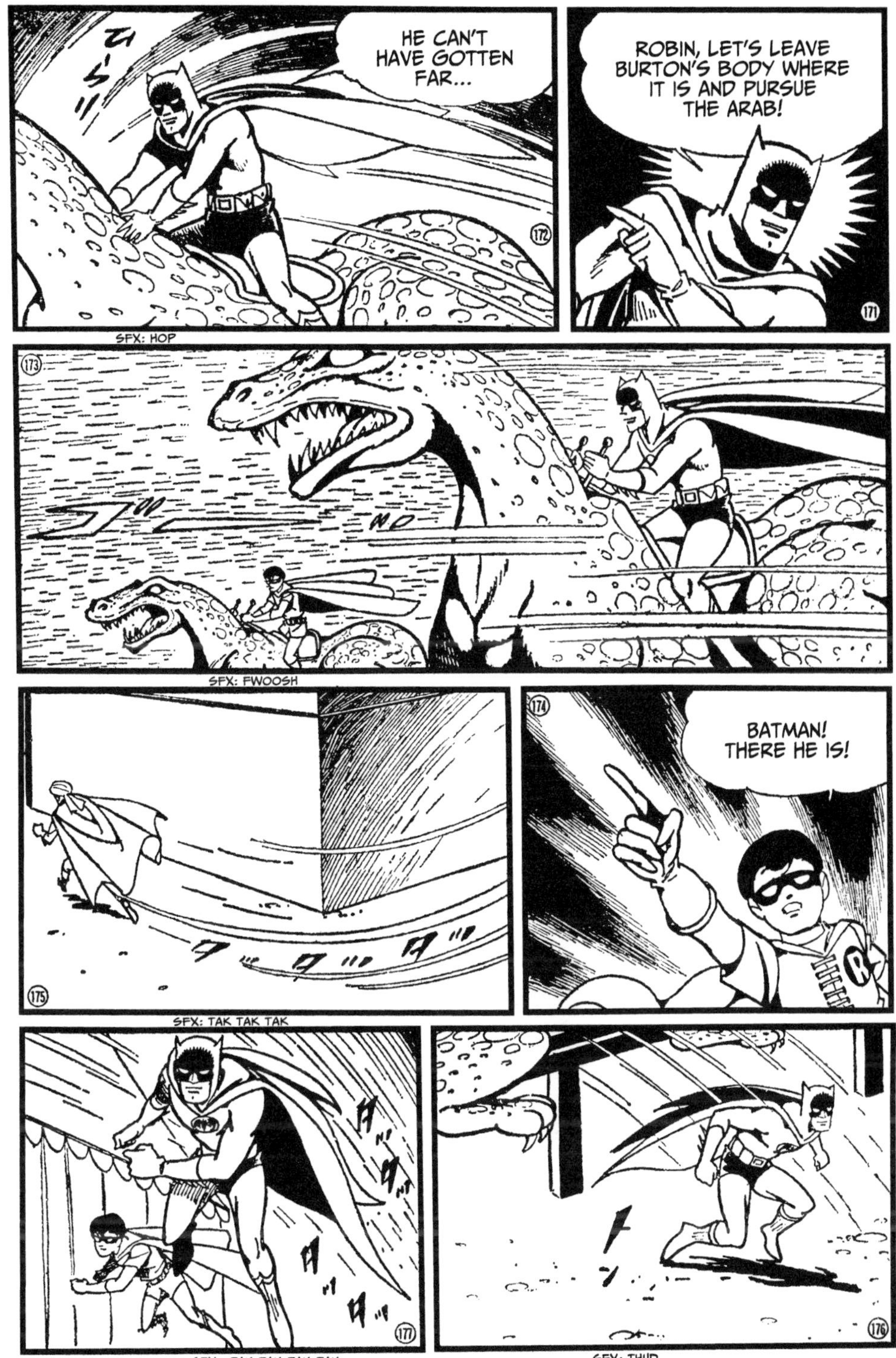
ROBIN, LET'S LEAVE BURTON'S BODY WHERE IT IS AND PURSUE THE ARAB!
HE CAN'T HAVE GOTTEN FAR...
SFX: HOP
SFX: FWOOSH
BATMAN! THERE HE IS!
SFX: TAK TAK TAK
SFX: THUD
SFX: TAK TAK TAK TAK

=CHUCKLE=... THAT'S RIGHT, WALK RIGHT IN FRONT OF THIS. THAT'LL BE THE END OF THE DYNAMIC DUO!

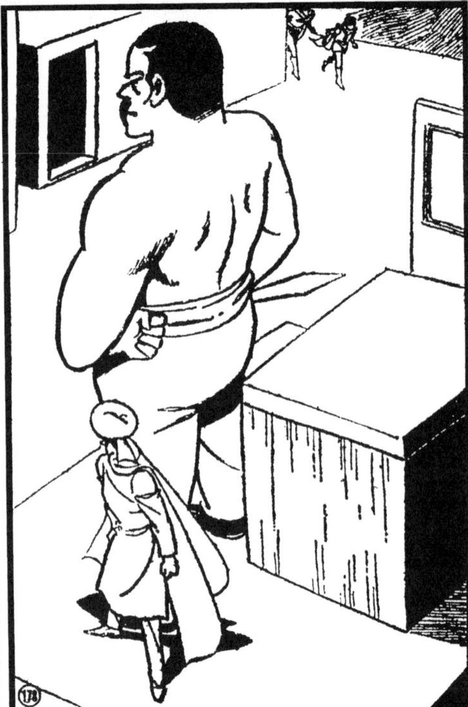

ROBIN, LOOK OUT!
AAAH!

SFX: WOBBLE

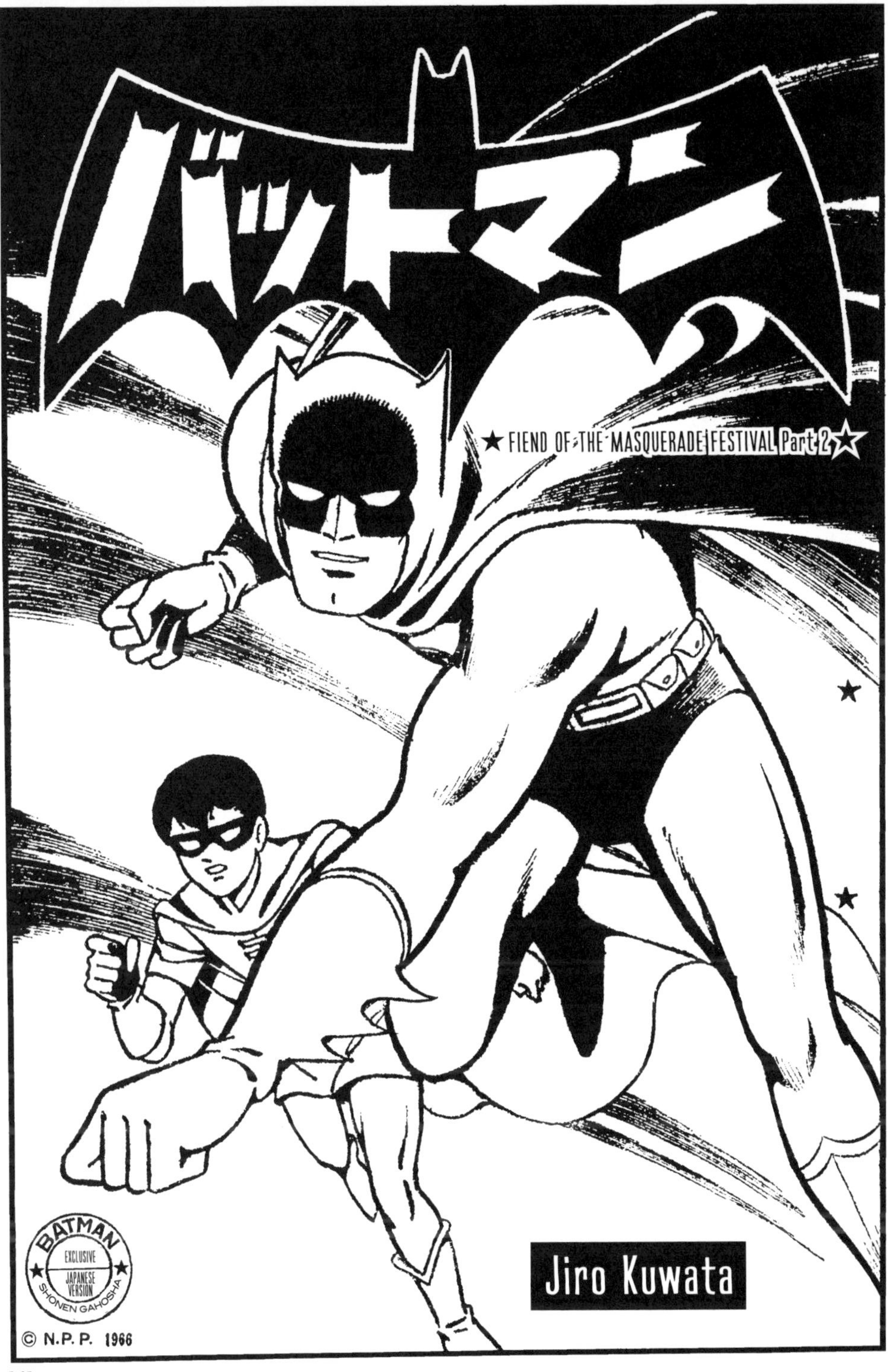
バットマン
★FIEND OF THE MASQUERADE FESTIVAL Part 2☆
BATMAN
EXCLUSIVE
JAPANESE VERSION
SHONEN GAHOSHA
Jiro Kuwata
© N.P.P. 1966

LAST EPISODE... Kelson, imprisoned for fencing stolen jewelry, broke out of jail. Batman and Robin learned that he was hiding in plain sight in the middle of a masquerade festival. However, someone murdered Kelson there with a poison blow dart. Luckily, photographer Vicki Vale was on the scene and happened to take a shot earlier of Kelson handing over a small package to a man dressed as a musketeer. The Dynamic Duo found the would-be musketeer and gave chase... until he was also murdered with a poison dart blown by a man wearing Arabian garb. Batman removed the musketeer's mask, revealing him as Burton, one of the security officers there. Batman and Robin chased after the Arab, but then a giant statue toppled towards the Boy Wonder!

⇦ Burton

Kelson ⇨

SFX: WOBBLE

ROBIN, LOOK OUT!

SFX: FWISH

SFX: CRUNCH

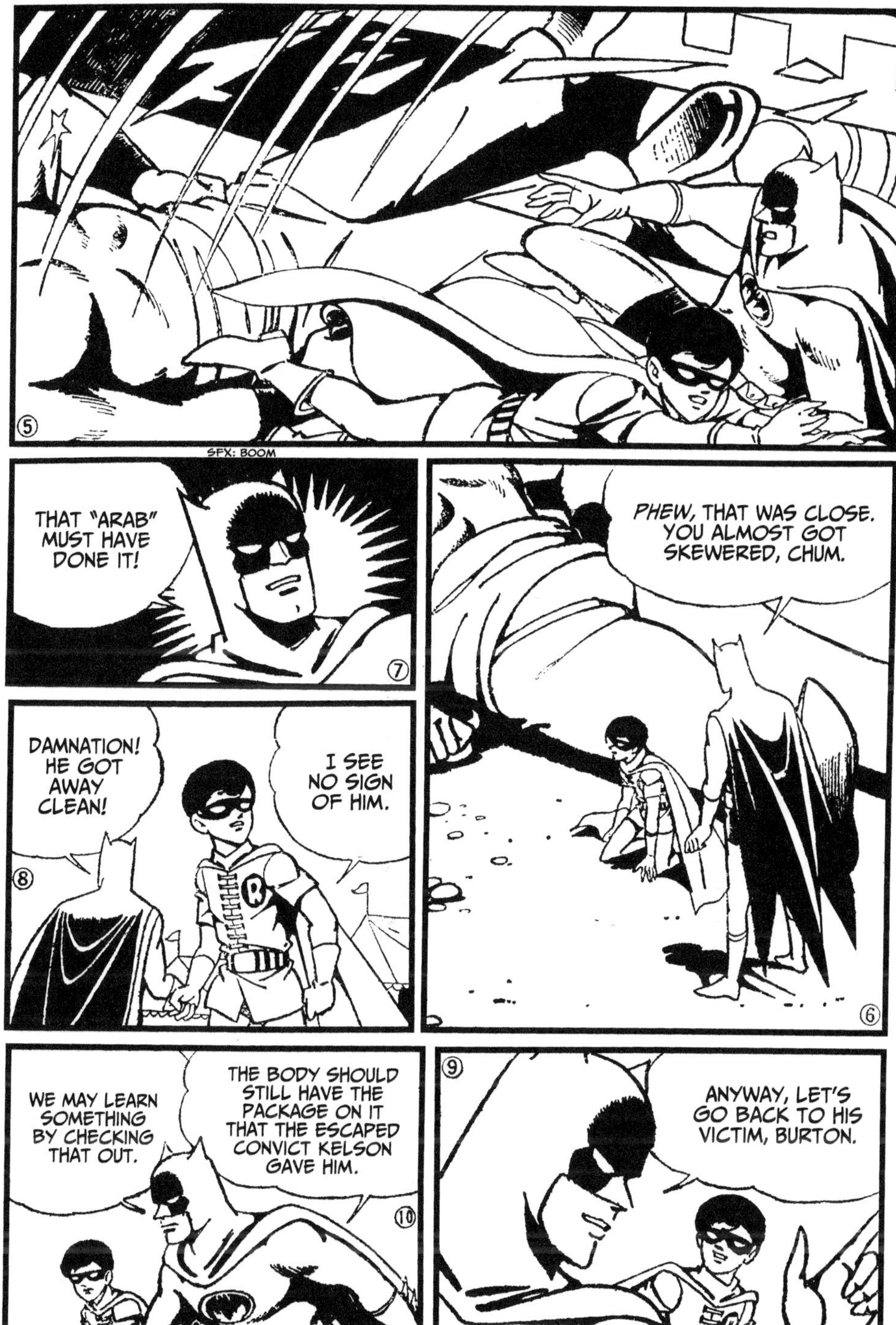

SFX: BOOM

PHEW, THAT WAS CLOSE. YOU ALMOST GOT SKEWERED, CHUM.

THAT "ARAB" MUST HAVE DONE IT!

I SEE NO SIGN OF HIM.
DAMNATION! HE GOT AWAY CLEAN!

ANYWAY, LET'S GO BACK TO HIS VICTIM, BURTON.

THE BODY SHOULD STILL HAVE THE PACKAGE ON IT THAT THE ESCAPED CONVICT KELSON GAVE HIM.
WE MAY LEARN SOMETHING BY CHECKING THAT OUT.

WHAT'S THIS? SOMEBODY STANDING NEXT TO BURTON'S CORPSE!

TOM DAWES, THE OTHER SECURITY OFFICER!

THAT CRUTCH...
I CAN IMAGINE IT DOUBLING AS A BLOW DART GUN.

I HAVE A HUNCH THAT TOM DAWES KILLED BOTH KELSON AND BURTON WITH THOSE POISON-TIPPED DARTS...

BATMAN! THE PACKAGE ISN'T HERE!
HMM...

TOM DAWES WAS WITH THE BODY WHEN WE GOT HERE. HE COULD EASILY HAVE PALMED THE PACKAGE...

AH!
SFX: YANK

W-WHAT ARE YOU DOING, BATMAN?

ROBIN! PAT HIM DOWN! THEN WE'LL KNOW WHETHER HE'S GOT THE PACKAGE OR NOT.

WHAT ARE YOU TALKING ABOUT? I DIDN'T TOUCH BURTON'S BODY!

LOOKS LIKE HE'S TELLING THE TRUTH. I DIDN'T FIND ANYTHING ON HIM.
...

THEN MAYBE BURTON HID THE PACKAGE SOMEWHERE BEFORE HE GOT KILLED?

LET'S TOSS HIS ROOM!

SFX: RUSTLE RUSTLE
BATMAN, I FOUND A STRANGE MAP!
SFX: RIFLE RIFLE

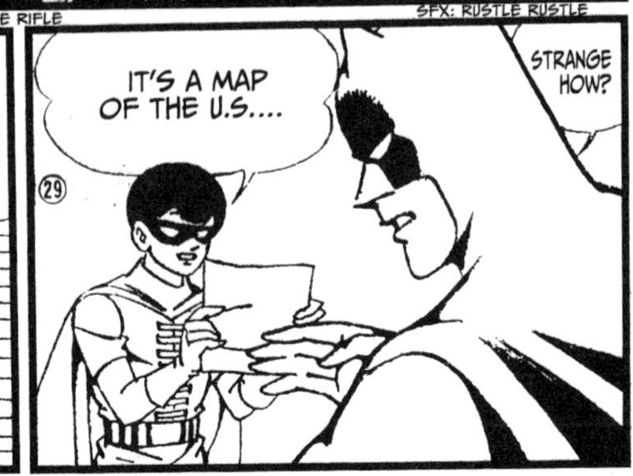
STRANGE HOW?
IT'S A MAP OF THE U.S....

...BUT SOMEBODY USED A PEN TO CIRCLE PLACES HERE AND THERE.
I SEE...

HMM... AND THERE ARE DOODLES NEXT TO EACH CIRCLE.
FOR BOSTON, THERE'S A UNICORN. FOR CHICAGO, A DRAGON...

MAYBE IT'S SOME KIND OF CODE?
THEY'RE ALL DOODLES OF MYTHOLOGICAL CREATURES...

THERE'S ONE PLACE HERE THAT COULD HAVE UNICORN AND DRAGON FIGURES.
THE WAX MUSEUM!

EXACTLY. LET'S PAY IT A VISIT.

SIGN: HOUSE OF WAX

FORTUNATELY, NOBODY ELSE IS HERE.
WE CAN SNEAK IN.

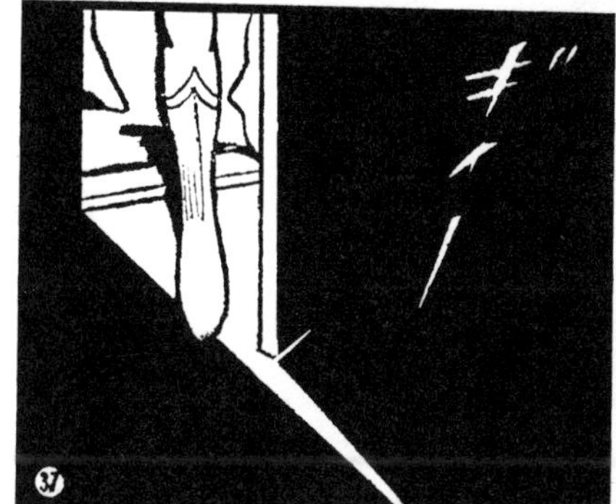
SFX: CREAK

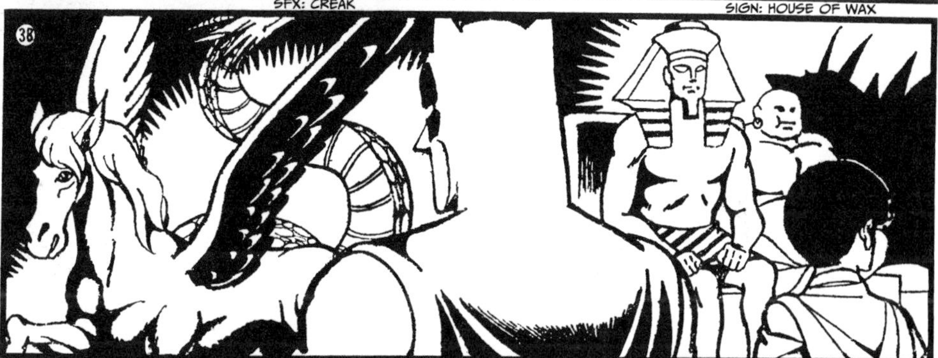

THERE'S A UNICORN, BATMAN!

HMM...

BATMAN! THE UNICORN'S BACK OPENED!
MM... EVIDENTLY, THERE'S A CONTRIVANCE IN THE HORN.
SFX: POP

HUH? THERE'S SOMETHING GLOWING INSIDE...

A DIAMOND NECKLACE...

ROBIN, THIS NECKLACE WAS STOLEN IN BOSTON!

COME TO THINK OF IT, THE UNICORN DOODLE WAS RIGHT NEXT TO BOSTON ON THAT MAP!

THAT'S RIGHT. THE MAP MUST BE A KEY, TELLING WHERE SOMETHING WAS STOLEN AND WHERE IT'S HIDDEN.

MOREOVER, ALL THE PLACES MARKED ON THE MAP WERE VISITED BY THE MASQUERADE FESTIVAL.

A GANG OF THIEVES MUST BE USING THE FESTIVAL AS A FRONT.
BURTON PROBABLY BOUGHT STOLEN MERCHANDISE FROM THEM AND SOLD IT FOR A PROFIT AT A DIFFERENT LOCATION, BUT WAS KILLED FOR HIS BETRAYAL.

SAY, THERE'S SOMETHING ELSE THAT'S GLOWING INSIDE THE UNICORN.

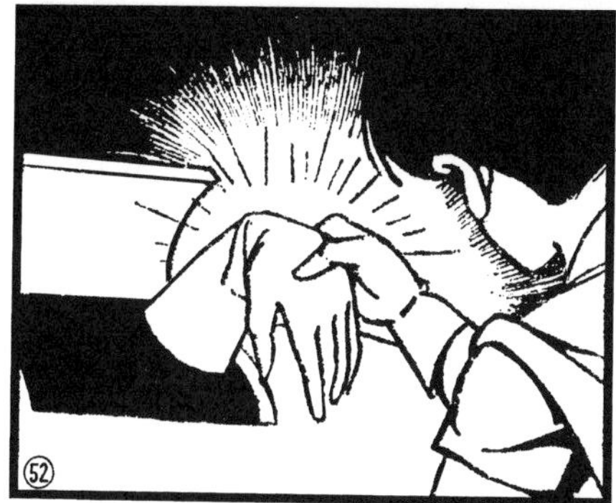

A GLOWING GLOVE...

WAIT. THERE'S LUMINOUS PAINT ON IT.

A GLOVE BESMIRCHED WITH LUMINOUS PAINT TELLS US THE WEARER TOUCHED SOMETHING THAT WAS COVERED IN FRESH LUMINOUS PAINT.

AND WHAT USES LUMINOUS PAINT HERE?

THE HAUNTED HOUSE! THEY MUST GO THROUGH GALLONS OF THAT STUFF IN THERE!

THEN LET'S GO.
IT FEELS LIKE ALL THE PIECES OF THIS MYSTERY ARE STARTING TO FALL INTO PLACE.

おばけやし

SIGN: HAUNTED HOUSE

HERE!

THE FESTIVAL'S CLOSED FOR THE NIGHT, SO THERE SHOULDN'T BE ANYONE INSIDE.

SFX: CACKLE CACKLE CACKLE

SHEESH. DON'T SCARE ME...

AAAHH!
SFX: SHRIEK

PHEW...
THERE'S NOTHING TO BE SCARED OF. IT'S ALL MAKE-BELIEVE.

I CAN GO UP AGAINST A DOZEN GANG MEMBERS WITHOUT BLINKING, BUT LOOKS LIKE THIS STUFF IS MY ACHILLES' HEEL.

AH!

LOOK AT THAT. THERE'S ONLY ONE PLACE THAT DOESN'T GLOW IN THE DARK.

THE LUMINOUS PAINT RUBBED OFF ONTO THAT GLOVE.
SO THEN THAT PACKAGE IS INSIDE OF IT...

I BELIEVE SO...

VOILÀ!

WHAT'S INSIDE?
LET'S SEE...

HMM...PLATES TO COUNTERFEIT PAPER MONEY.

IT'S WELL-MADE.
THE THIEVES MUST HAVE FIGURED THEY'D MAKE A BUNDLE USING THIS.

?

SFX: CREAK CREAK

AAAH!

SFX: CREAK CREAK

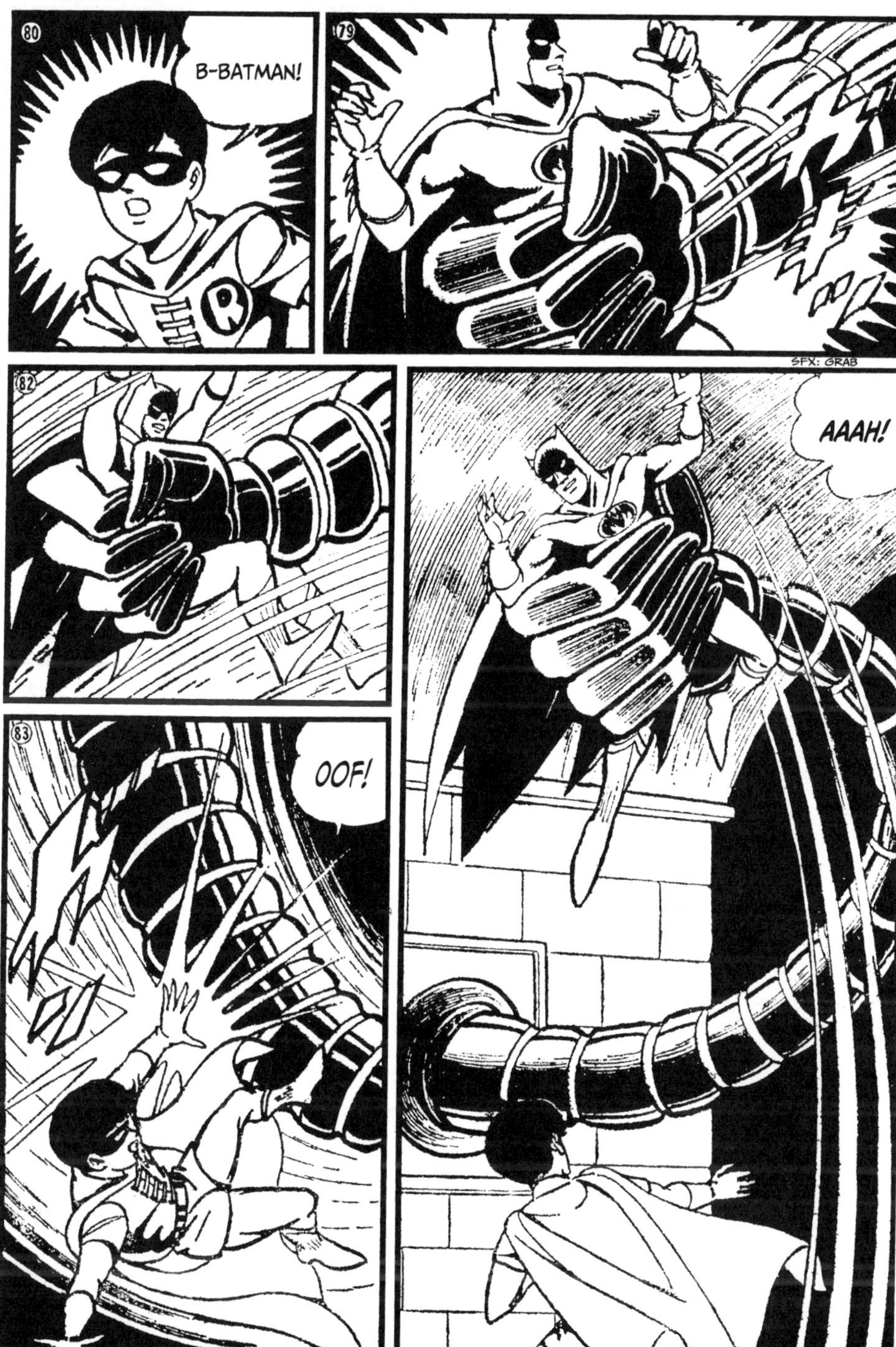
SFX: GRAB
B-BATMAN!
AAAH!
OOF!
SFX: KRAK

SFX: WHUMP
SFX: CRASH
ROBIN! THERE SHOULD BE A SWITCH ON THE SIDE OF THE WALL! TURN THIS MACHINE OFF!
SFX: TAK TAK

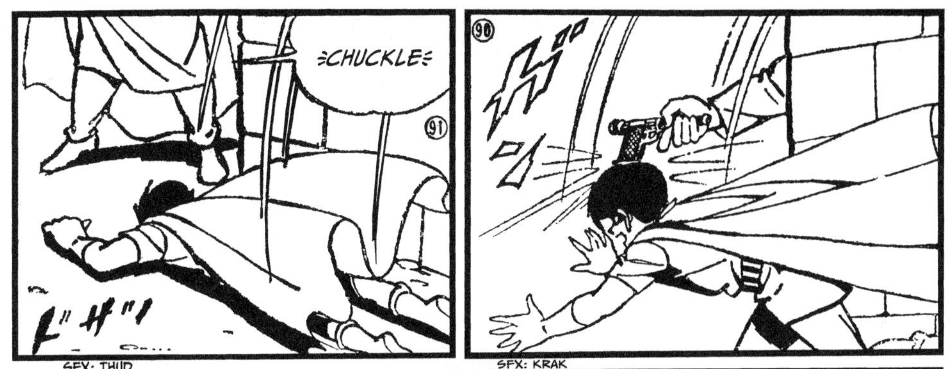
≈CHUCKLE≈

SFX: KRAK

SFX: THUD

AH! YOU! THE ARAB!

≈CHUCKLE≈ YOU'VE LEARNED TOO MUCH, BATMAN.

BUT THEN AGAIN, AS THEY SAY, DEAD MEN TELL NO TALES...

バットマン
★FIEND OF THE MASQUERADE FESTIVAL Part 3★
BATMAN
EXCLUSIVE
JAPANESE VERSION
SHONEN GAHOSHA
© N. P. P. 1967
Jiro Kuwata

LAST EPISODE...

Two people were murdered at the Masquerade Festival. Investigating one of the victims, Burton, led Batman and Robin to the haunted house, where they found his mystery package. Inside were plates to counterfeit paper money. Just then, a giant mechanical hand attached to a wall grabbed Batman and picked him up. And the murderer dressed in Arabian garb stepped out of the shadows...

≡CHUCKLE≡ AND YOU'RE THE GREAT BATMAN, HELPLESS AS A BABY!

Y-YOU! THE "ARAB"!

IT SEEMS YOU DIDN'T NOTICE MY HIDDEN PRESENCE IN THE WAX MUSEUM.

MM...SO YOU OVERHEARD OUR CONVERSATION AND CAME HERE TO AMBUSH US, EH?

≡CHUCKLE≡ PRECISELY.

I'VE KILLED TWO PEOPLE ALREADY. CAN YOU GUESS THE IDENTITY OF MY THIRD VICTIM?

YOU, BATMAN!

...

WHEN I TURN THIS WHEEL...

SFX: CREAK

SFX: WHAM

SFX: WHOOSH

SFX: SWOOSH

SFX: WHUD

HA HAHAHA HA!

SFX: SMASH

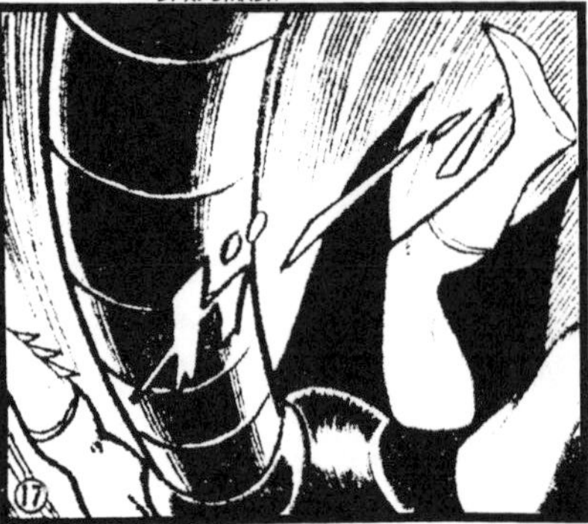

SFX: WHAK

=CHUCKLE= YOU'RE LIKE A LIMP RAG DOLL.

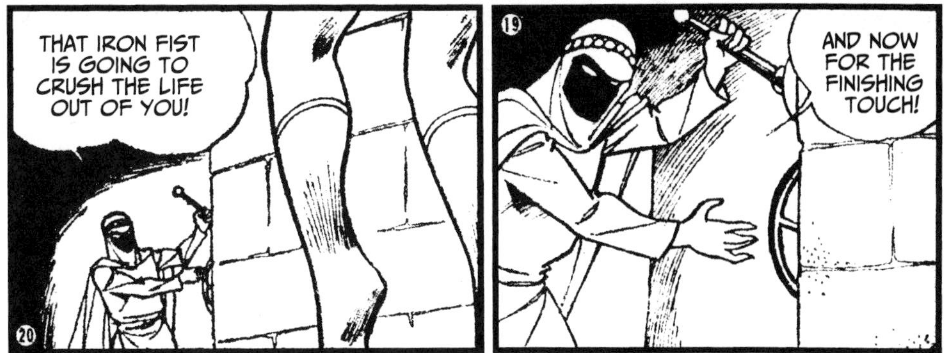
AND NOW FOR THE FINISHING TOUCH!
THAT IRON FIST IS GOING TO CRUSH THE LIFE OUT OF YOU!

SFX: YANK

ARRR GGH...
SFX: CRUSH

UNNH... HAVE TO...DO SOMETHING OR I REALLY WILL BE CRUSHED!

YES, YOU CERTAINLY WILL! IN JUST A MOMENT, I PREDICT YOUR RIBS WILL CRACK LIKE TOOTHPICKS.

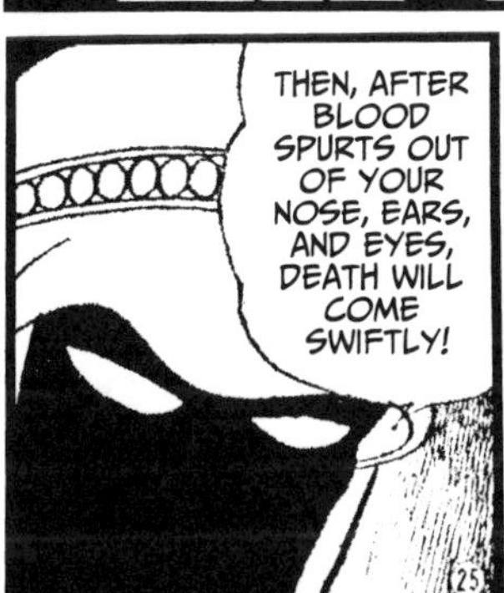
THEN, AFTER BLOOD SPURTS OUT OF YOUR NOSE, EARS, AND EYES, DEATH WILL COME SWIFTLY!

THE FIEND! MUST BE SOME WAY OUT OF THIS PINCH...

HAHAHA! THERE IS NOTHING YOU CAN DO INSIDE OF THAT IRON GRIP!
ONE MORE SQUEEZE SHOULD DO IT!

OH, THAT'S RIGHT! I STILL HAVE THE PLATES!

SFX: FWISH

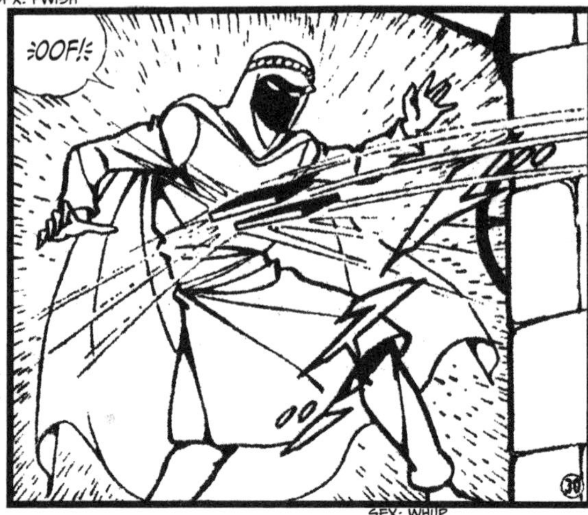
OOF!

SFX: WHUP

OOGH...

GETTING HIM AWAY FROM THAT LEVER HAS MADE THE IRON HAND LOOSEN ITS GRIP...

YES! JUST ENOUGH WIGGLE ROOM FOR ME TO REACH MY UTILITY BELT!

SFX: FWISH FWISH

SFX: FWISH

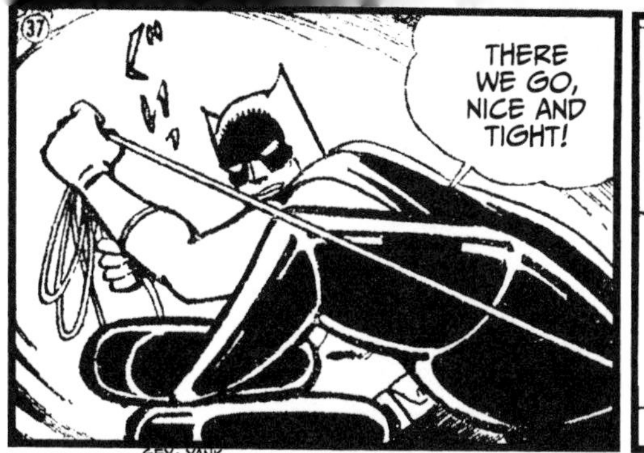
THERE WE GO, NICE AND TIGHT!

SFX: YANK

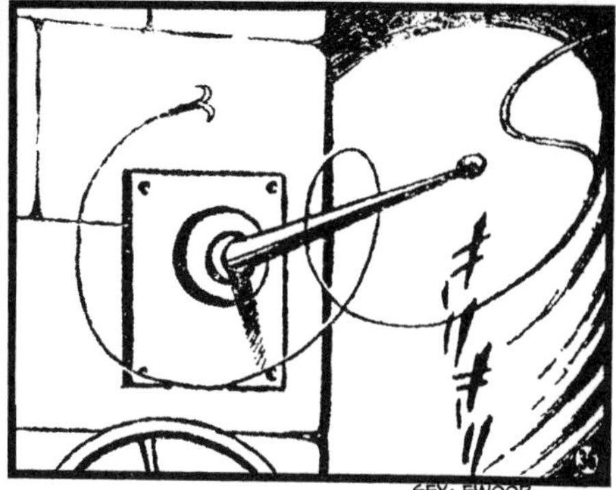

SFX: FWOOP

IT WORKED! THE HAND OPENED!

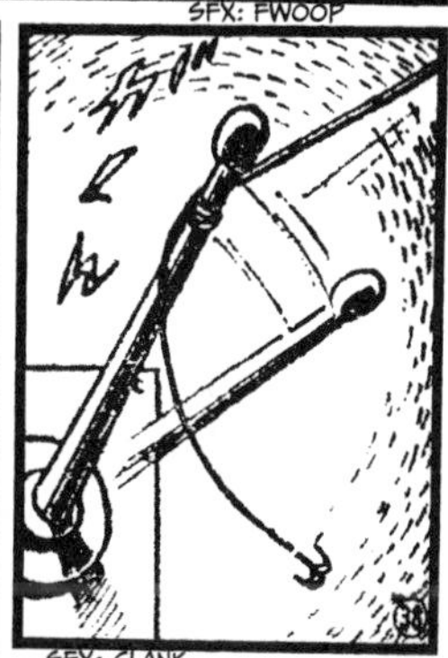

SFX: CLANK

SFX: SWISH

ROBIN!
UNNH...

ARE YOU OKAY?
YEAH, I'M FINE.
WHERE'S THE ARAB?

SFX: TWEET

OH! HE BLEW A WHISTLE. WHICH IS A SIGN FOR WHAT?

A SIGN FOR *THEM*, BATMAN!

YEAH. HENCHMEN...

SFX: BRAAAAP BRAAP

SFX: TAT TAT

SFX: FWISH

?
THROW A TOY AT ME?!
SFX: BRAAAP
SFX: BOOM
? ?
GROAN...
SFX: WHUMP
SFX: THUD
THE NUMBSKULLS. THEY DON'T EVEN KNOW ENOUGH NOT TO FIRE AT A KNOCKOUT BOMB!
BATMAN! THE ARAB IS GETTING AWAY!

OR IS HE?!

AAAH!

EEE YAAAA!

NOW THE HAND'S ON THE OTHER FOOT!

AIEEE!

SFX: KRAK

SFX: WHOMP

WELL, WELL. APPARENTLY, YOU DON'T HAVE ANY STAYING POWER...

ぽい

SFX: WHUMP

SFX: TOSS

GET UP! IT'S TIME TO LEARN YOUR TRUE IDENTITY!
GROAN...

WHO DO YOU THINK HE IS, ROBIN?

WHY, TOM DAWES, OF COURSE!

DAWES SAID HE USED A CRUTCH BECAUSE OF SOME LEG INJURY, BUT I BET IT'S A BLOWGUN IN DISGUISE!

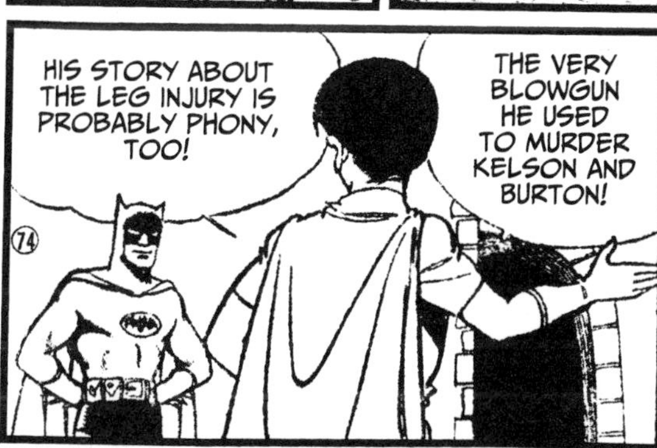
THE VERY BLOWGUN HE USED TO MURDER KELSON AND BURTON!
HIS STORY ABOUT THE LEG INJURY IS PROBABLY PHONY, TOO!

SO I SAY WE'LL SEE THE MUG OF TOM DAWES WHEN YOU RIP OFF THE MASK.

I SEE...
WELL, ONLY ONE WAY TO FIND OUT...

HEY!
AH! CHIEF GORDON!
SFX: THUD THUD THUD
I CAME RUNNING OVER AS SOON AS I HEARD!
HEARD? WHO CALLED YOU, CHIEF?
I DID.
EH?
TOM DAWES!
THEN THE ARAB IS...

CAN I GET A DRUM ROLL?

SFX: SWISH

AH! HIM?!
YOUR DEDUCTIONS WERE OFF THE MARK, ROBIN.
SORRY, CHUM.

THE "ARAB" IS ASHLEY, THE GUY WHO RUNS THE MASQUERADE FESTIVAL!

I'D SUSPECTED TOM DAWES MYSELF EARLIER.

BUT I LOOKED INTO HIS INJURY AND THAT CRUTCH WHEN I HAD A MINUTE, AND IT ALL CHECKED OUT.

I'M SORRY I SUSPECTED YOU OF A DOUBLE MURDER, TOM.
OH, IT'S UNDERSTANDABLE.

I'M JUST GLAD YOU TWO PUT AN END TO THIS MESS.
BUT I AM SHOCKED THAT MY EMPLOYER, ASHLEY, AND PARTNER, BURTON, TURNED OUT TO BE BAD GUYS.

WHY DID YOU KILL KELSON AND BURTON, ASHLEY?
T-THEY HAD IT COMING TO THEM!

KELSON WAS MY UNDERLING, A VERY CLEVER FELLOW.

AND I PAID HIM A HEFTY SUM TO CREATE THOSE COUNTERFEIT MONEY PLATES.

BUT HE WAS ARRESTED FOR FENCING STOLEN JEWELRY BEFORE I COULD TAKE POSSESSION. WHEN HE WENT TO JAIL, THE PLATES I PAID FOR WERE HIDDEN SOMEWHERE.

AND BURTON STABBED ME IN THE BACK. HE BROKE KELSON OUT OF PRISON ON HIS OWN WITH THE INTENTION OF GETTING HIS HANDS ON MY PLATES.

SO I MURDERED THEM BOTH!

HE'LL PROBABLY GET THE DEATH PENALTY.
THAT'S WHAT HAPPENS WHEN YOU MURDER TWO PEOPLE IN COLD BLOOD.

BATMAN!
OH, VICKI!

I HEARD YOU SOLVED THE CASE. CONGRAT-ULATIONS.

THANK YOU. I WOULDN'T HAVE BEEN ABLE TO DO IT WITHOUT THAT PHOTO YOU TOOK.

BATMAN! WOULD YOU BE THE KING OF THE MASQUERADE FESTIVAL?

THEN VICKI CAN BE MY QUEEN...
...AND ROBIN WILL BE THE PRINCE!

SFX: HURRAH!

バットマン
BATMAN
EXCLUSIVE JAPANESE VERSION
SHONEN GAHOSHA
© N. P. P. 1967
★MYSTERY OF THE OUTSIDER★
HAPPY NEW YEAR!
JIRO KUWATA

SFX: WHOOSH
SFX: VROOO
SFX: BUDDA-BUDDA-BUDDA
SFX: ZING ZING
SFX: WHOOSH
BATMAN! THEY ESCAPED INTO DEATH VALLEY!
THEN THEY'LL BE TRAPPED LIKE THE RATS THAT THEY ARE!

SFX: BEEP BEEP BEEP

Meanwhile, a certain alarm goes off in the Batcave...

YES, THIS IS BATMAN'S BUTLER.
OH, YES, CHIEF GORDON.

WELL, WHERE'S BATMAN?!
RIGHT NOW, IN PURSUIT OF THE RED LIZARD GANG.

WHAT?! DON'T TELL ME THEY ESCAPED TO DEATH VALLEY!

PLEASE HOLD A MOMENT. I'LL CHECK THE CURRENT LOCATION OF THE BATMOBILE.

AH!
SFX: BEEP BEEP

IT SEEMS THE BATMOBILE IS INDEED IN THE AREA OF DEATH VALLEY.
IS SOMETHING AMISS, CHIEF GORDON?

I'LL SAY! THE RED LIZARD GANG LAID A TRAP IN DEATH VALLEY!

EH?! THEN BATMAN AND ROBIN WILL...

I MUST WARN THEM!

BUT I HAVE NO MEANS... WHAT SHALL I DO...?

THAT'S IT! I'LL GO TO DEATH VALLEY MYSELF!
I ONLY PRAY THAT I'LL BE IN TIME...

SFX: VRRRR

PLEASE BE SAFE!

THEY'RE OUT OF PLACES TO RUN, SO NOW THEY'RE JUST HOLED UP IN THERE.
STILL, BE CAREFUL, ROBIN. REMEMBER, THEY'VE GOT A MACHINE GUN.

I'LL SEND OUT A BATCAMERA.

SFX: FWISH

SFX: FWISH

THIS SCREEN ATTACHED TO MY BELT SHOWS WHATEVER THE CAMERA SEES.

WHAT?!

WHAT IS IT?
THEIR CAR IS EMPTY!

THEY'RE GONE...

HOW DID THEY SLIP AWAY?
LET'S CHECK IT OUT.

THEY REALLY ARE GONE!

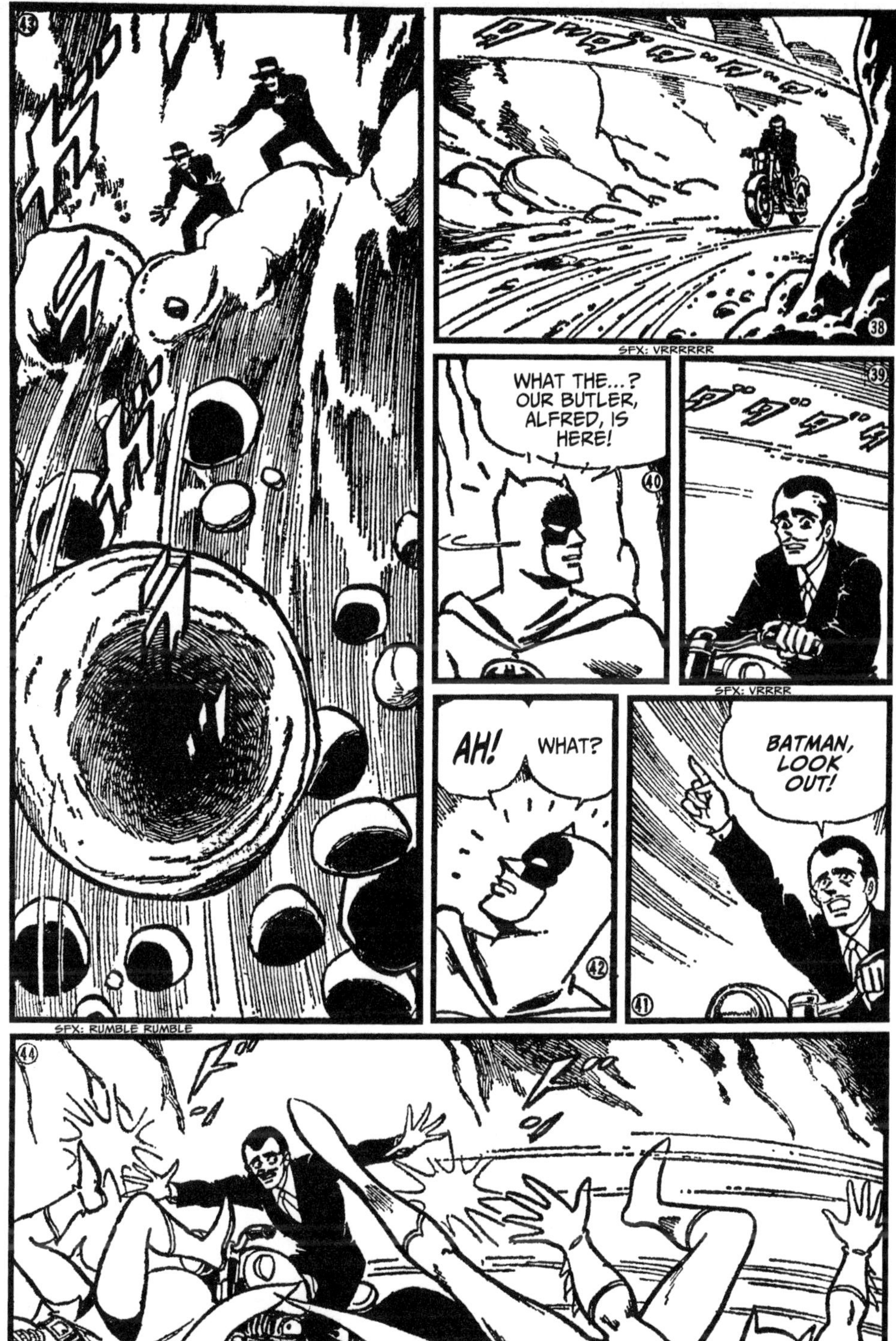
SFX: VRRRRRR
WHAT THE...? OUR BUTLER, ALFRED, IS HERE!
SFX: VRRRR
BATMAN, LOOK OUT!
AH!
WHAT?
SFX: RUMBLE RUMBLE
SFX: SHOVE SHOVE

SFX: RUMBLE RUMBLE

AH! ALFRED!

H-HE'S DEAD...

Shortly afterwards, a police squad led by Gordon arrived and captured every last member of the Red Lizard gang. However, it was too late for Alfred, who sacrificed his own life to save Batman and Robin...

His body was placed in a refrigerated coffin and laid to rest in the Wayne family crypt.

But neither Batman nor Robin knew what would happen that night at the cemetery. And therein lies this tale...
ウェイン家墓地
SIGN: WAYNE FAMILY CRYPT
What's going to happen, you ask? Observe...
SFX: CRUNCH CRUNCH
This man's name is Crawford. The world doesn't know it, but he's a brilliant scientist.
MMM...I CAN HEAR EVERYTHING! I HEAR EVERYTHING CLEARLY WITH THESE SUPER AUDITORY ENHANCERS.

IT'S AN UNQUALIFIED SUCCESS! I CAN EVEN HEAR THE BEATING OF INSECT WINGS!

CHALK UP ANOTHER INVENTION FROM ME.

MM? WHAT'S THAT?
SOMEONE MOANING...?

IT'S COMING FROM WITHIN THAT CRYPT...
ウエイン家

SIGN: WAYNE FAMILY

WAIT, HUMAN MOANING INSIDE A CRYPT?

THIS IS THE LAST PLACE I'D EXPECT TO FIND A LIVING PERSON, BUT...
家墓地

SIGN: FAMILY CRYPT

SFX: CREAK

SFX: TAK TAK

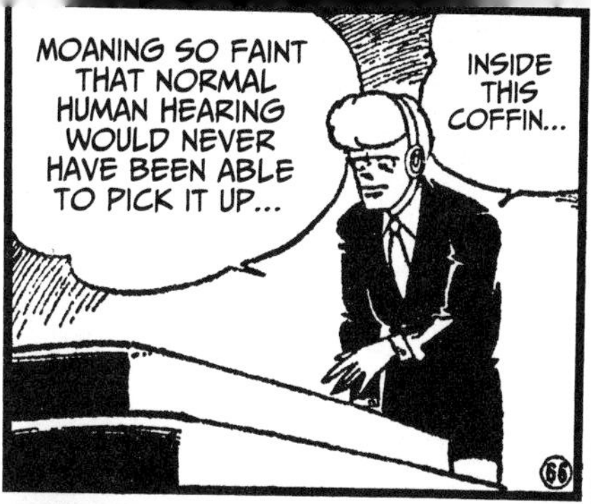

INSIDE THIS COFFIN...
MOANING SO FAINT THAT NORMAL HUMAN HEARING WOULD NEVER HAVE BEEN ABLE TO PICK IT UP...

...BUT IT COMES IN LOUD AND CLEAR WITH MY SUPER AUDITORY ENHANCERS!

GROAN...

I CAN HEAR IT! THIS MAN IS STILL ALIVE!

MUST SAVE BATMAN AND ROBIN...
MUST SAVE BATMAN AND ROBIN...

HE'S DESPERATELY CLINGING TO LIFE! WILLPOWER ALONE IS KEEPING HIM ALIVE!

THAT'S RIGHT... I INVENTED A CELLULAR REGENERATION MACHINE AND TRIED TO BRING CORPSES BACK TO LIFE SEVERAL TIMES, BUT MY EXPERIMENTS ENDED IN FAILURE.

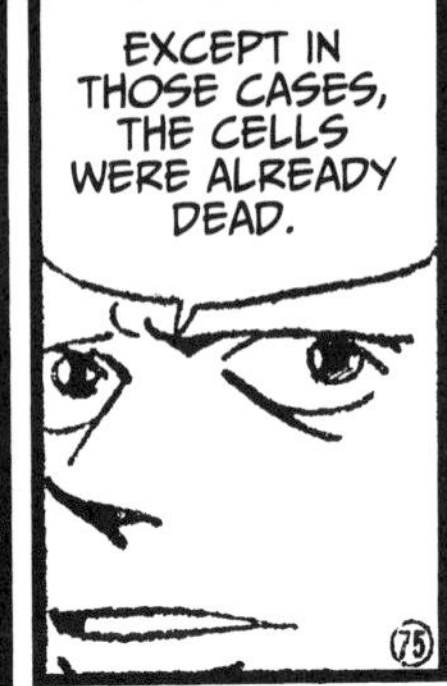
EXCEPT IN THOSE CASES, THE CELLS WERE ALREADY DEAD.

I MAY BE ABLE TO BRING THIS MAN BACK.
NO, I *KNOW* I CAN DO IT!

HE'S BEYOND HELP FROM ANY DOCTOR...
...BUT HE'S GOT A CHANCE WITH ME!

地
I'LL TAKE HIM BACK TO MY LABORATORY.

SIGN: CRYPT

Crawford loaded Alfred's body into the car and drove to a house on the outskirts of the city...

MAINSTREAM SCIENTISTS DON'T UNDERSTAND MY GENIUS! THEY TREAT ME LIKE A FREAK!

BUT THIS TIME I'LL SHOW THEM JUST HOW BRILLIANT I AM!

Scientific devices cluttered the basement laboratory...

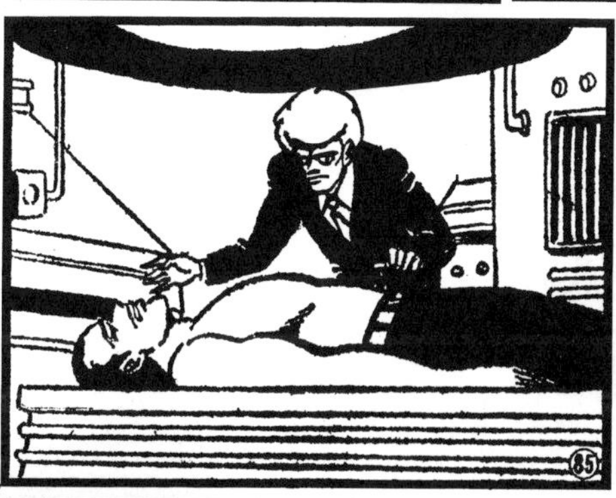

WILL I FINALLY HAVE SUCCESS WITH MY CELLULAR REGENERATION MACHINE?

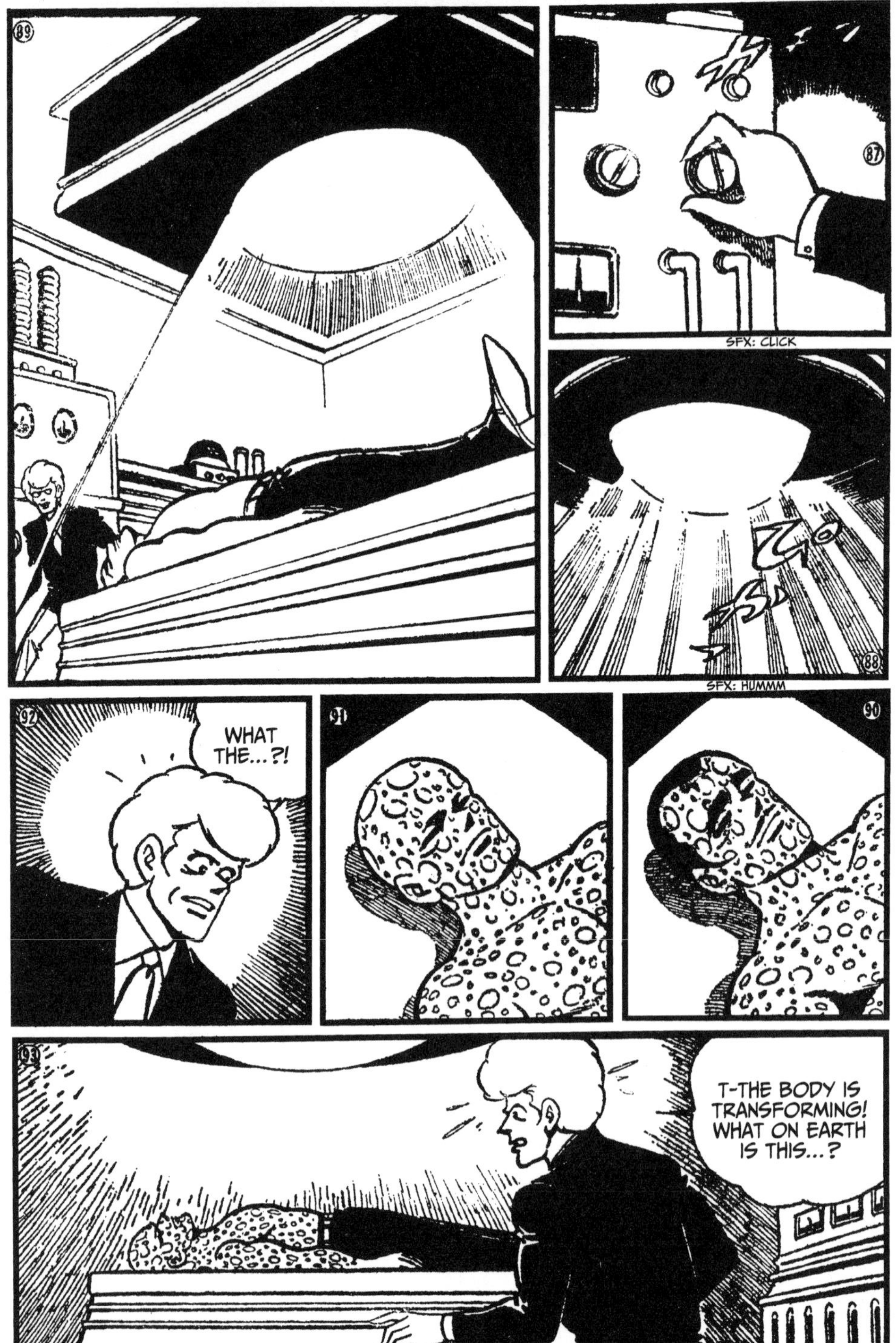
SFX: CLICK
SFX: HUMMM
WHAT THE...?!
T-THE BODY IS TRANSFORMING! WHAT ON EARTH IS THIS...?

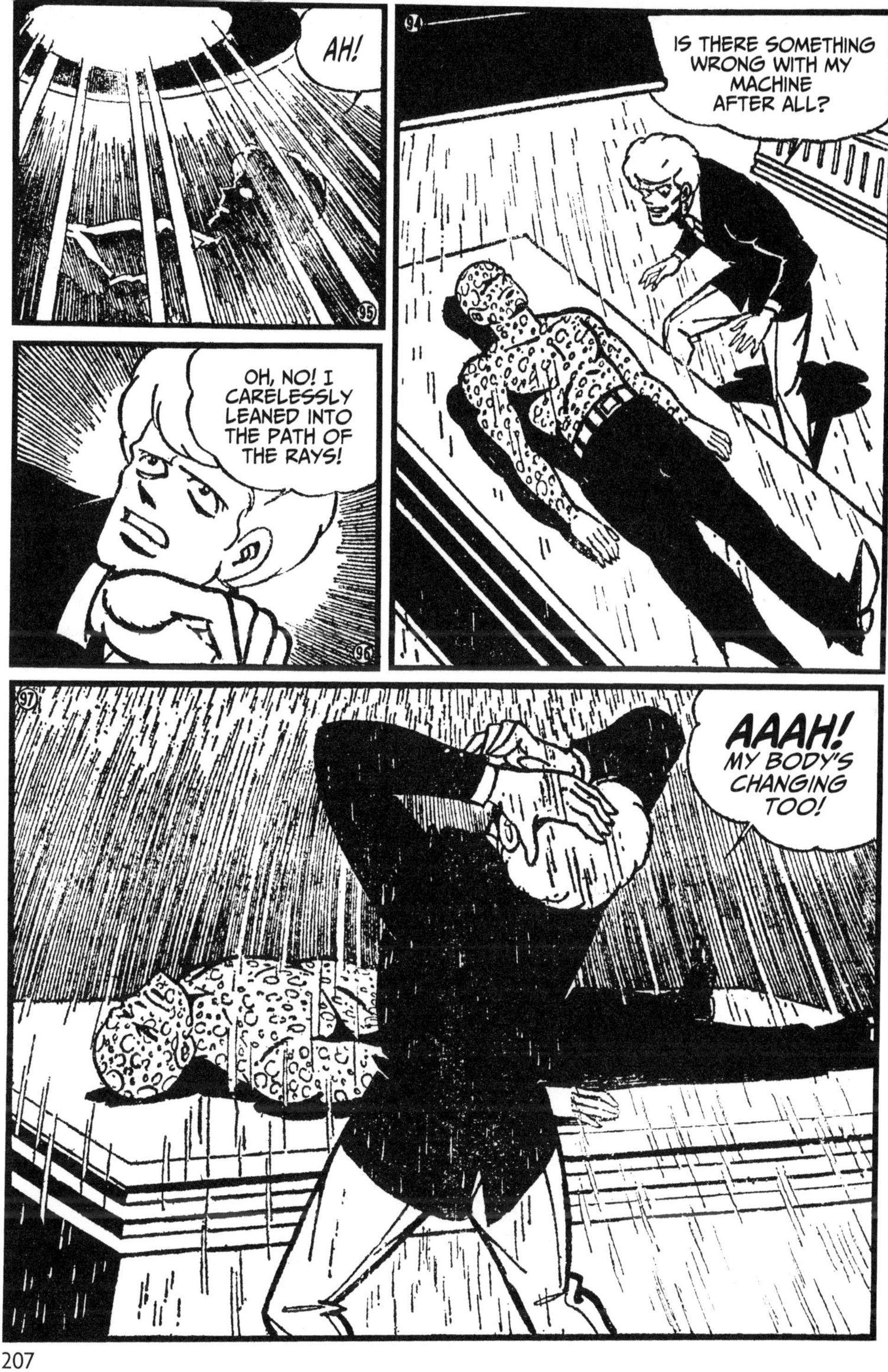

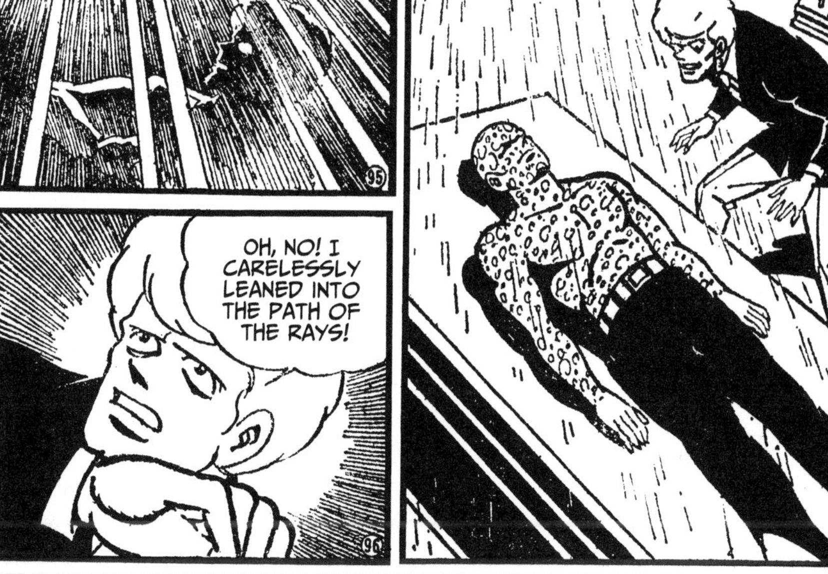
IS THERE SOMETHING WRONG WITH MY MACHINE AFTER ALL?
OH, NO! I CARELESSLY LEANED INTO THE PATH OF THE RAYS!

AH!

AAAH! MY BODY'S CHANGING TOO!

バットマン
★MYSTERY OF THE OUTSIDER Part 2★
BATMAN
EXCLUSIVE
JAPANESE VERSION
SHONEN GAHOSHA
© N. P. P. 1967
Jiro Kuwata

LAST EPISODE...

Bruce Wayne's butler, Alfred, died while saving Batman and Robin. That night, a lone man appeared in a graveyard and carried Alfred's body away. He is Crawford, a scientist whose name is unknown to the world at large. Crawford laid Alfred's body on a slab under his cell regeneration machine and flipped a switch. Alfred's form began to change before Crawford's eyes...

AAAH! MY BODY'S CHANGING, TOO!

EEEYAAAAA!

SFX: WHUMP

≈GROAN≈...

W-WHAT HAPPENED?
I'M ALIVE AGAIN...

AND I FEEL LIKE THIS IS MY HOME...

THIS IS THE FIRST TIME I'VE SEEN SO MANY MACHINES...

...AND YET, I KNOW HOW THEY WORK.

THIS IS ALSO THE FIRST TIME I'VE SEEN THAT MAN, BUT I KNOW EVERYTHING ABOUT HIM.

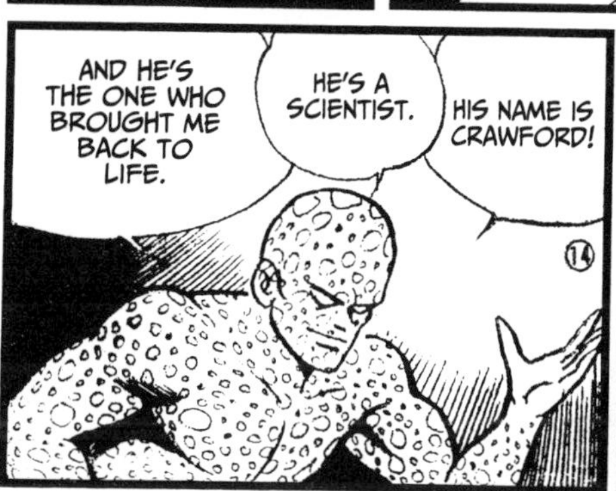
HIS NAME IS CRAWFORD!
HE'S A SCIENTIST.
AND HE'S THE ONE WHO BROUGHT ME BACK TO LIFE.

MM?

WHAT?! HIS FACE HAS TURNED INTO MY FORMER FACE!

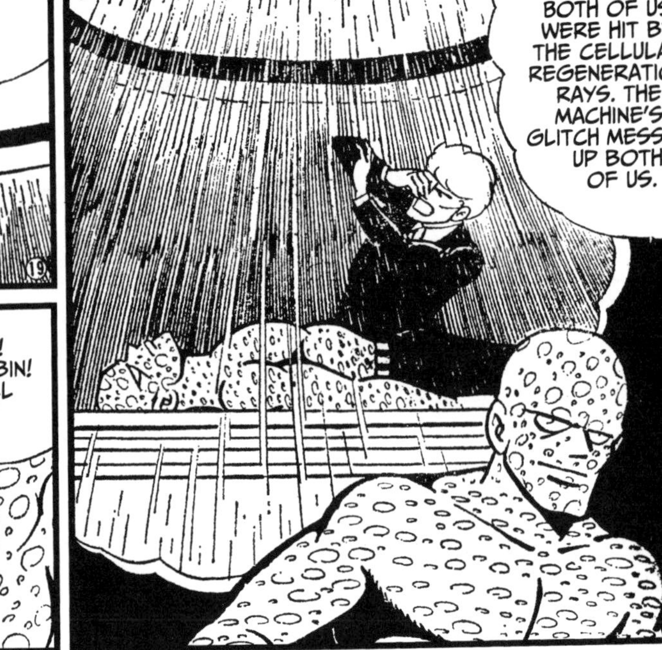
I SEE... BOTH OF US WERE HIT BY THE CELLULAR REGENERATION RAYS. THE MACHINE'S GLITCH MESSED UP BOTH OF US.
THAT'S RIGHT! BATMAN AND ROBIN! I NEED TO KILL THEM BOTH!

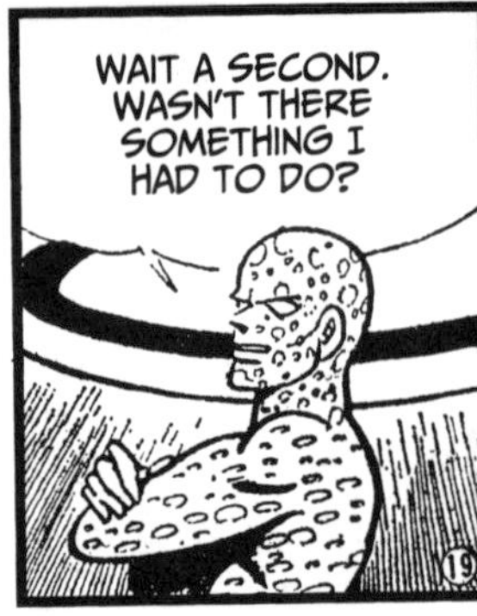
WAIT A SECOND. WASN'T THERE SOMETHING I HAD TO DO?

BUT BEFORE I MURDER THE DYNAMIC DUO, I HAVE TO GUARD AGAINST PRYING EYES BY MAKING IT LOOK LIKE NOTHING HAPPENED HERE...

Until now, Alfred has always aided Batman and Robin in their crusade for justice. But those feelings of loyalty and duty have been turned upside down by the defective cellular regeneration machine...

AH, YES. FIRST, I'LL TAKE THIS MAN TO THE CEMETERY.

SO EVEN IF BATMAN INVESTIGATES THERE, HE'LL FIND "ME" AND BE NONE THE WISER!

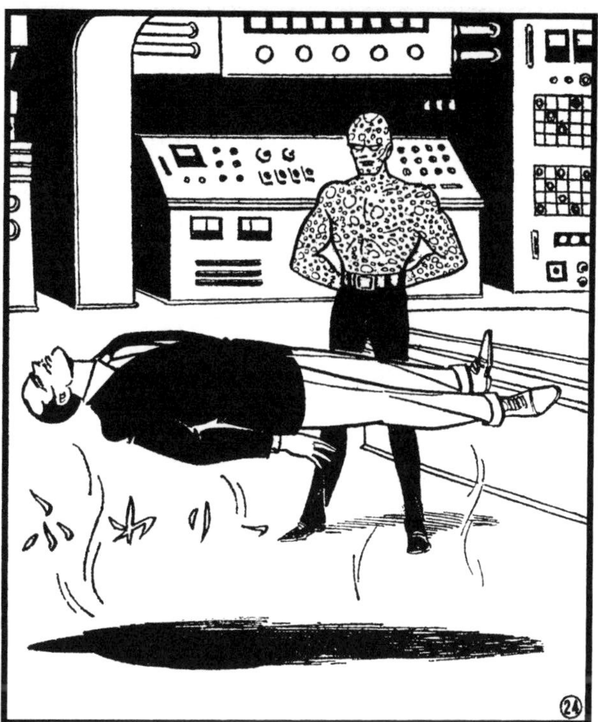
24

SFX: FLOAT

CHUCKLE
IT SEEMS MY MIRACULOUS RESURRECTION IS ACCOMPANIED BY ASTOUNDING PSIONIC ABILITIES.
25

ANYTHING THAT I'VE TOUCHED...
26

27
...IS UNDER MY COMPLETE CONTROL.

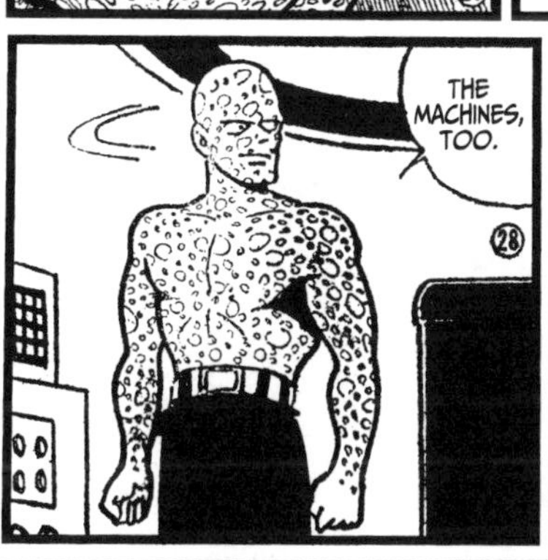
THE MACHINES, TOO.
28

29

SFX: WEEEN

30
CHUCKLE

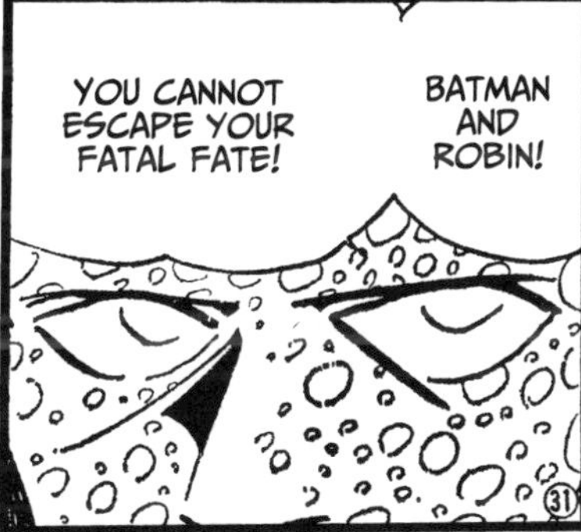
BATMAN AND ROBIN!
YOU CANNOT ESCAPE YOUR FATAL FATE!
31

This is the mansion of millionaire Bruce Wayne.
At first glance, it looks to be no more than the stately manor of a very wealthy person...

...but all manner of cutting-edge machinery is lined up in the huge cavern underneath the residence.

Like this nuclear reactor that fuels up the atomic-powered Batmobile...

This electronic computer...

This electronic memory device...

And the Batmobile itself, which the Dynamic Duo uses to tool around town and catch villains in the act!

OH, WHAT A BEAUTIFUL MORNING!
BIRD: CHIRP
BRUSH, BRUSH...
SFX: GARGLE GARGLE
SFX: CHIRP
?
SFX: VROOO
HUH? A TRUCK'S PULLED UP...
IT LOOKS LIKE A DELIVERY TRUCK.
GOOD MORNING, DICK!
BRUCE, DID YOU ORDER SOMETHING FROM A CATALOG?
NOT THAT I RECALL...

48
SFX: SKREEE

49
THAT'S STRANGE. I WONDER WHAT THEY BROUGHT OVER.
LET'S TAKE A CLOSER LOOK.

50

THEY'RE UNLOADING A BIG BOX.
51

52
SFX: WHUMP

53

HUH? TWO OF THEM...
54

SHOULD WE OPEN THEM?
I SUPPOSE SO...

SFX: RATTLE

SFX: FWISH

SAY, WHAT ARE THESE? WHO ORDERED YOU TO DELIVER THEM HERE?

HEY, HOLD UP A MINUTE, FELLA. I ASKED YOU A QUESTION!

SFX: SLAM

SFX: VROOOM

DO YOU BELIEVE THAT? GUY DROVE OFF WITHOUT A WORD...
ANYWAY, WE'LL GET OUR ANSWERS WHEN WE OPEN THESE THINGS.
TRUE, TRUE. WELL, LET'S GIVE 'EM THE OLD HEAVE-HO.
YOU KNOW, COME TO THINK OF IT, THIS BOX LOOKS AN AWFUL LOT LIKE A COFFIN.
AAAH!
W-WHAT IS THIS?!

B-BATMAN'S CORPSE...

NOT QUITE. LOOK CLOSELY.

IT'S A WAX DUMMY.

THEN WHAT'S IN THE OTHER COFFIN?

JUST AS I THOUGHT. A WAX DUMMY OF ROBIN.

WHO IN THE WORLD WOULD PLAY A PRANK LIKE THIS?

OH, IT'S NO PRANK.
IN FACT, THIS MAY BE SOMEONE'S WAY OF THROWING DOWN THE GAUNTLET.

BUT NOBODY KNOWS WE'RE BATMAN AND ROBIN!

ALMOST NOBODY. REMEMBER, THERE ARE TWO.

ONE IS CHIEF GORDON.

AND THERE'S NO WAY THAT CHIEF GORDON WOULD THROW DOWN A GAUNTLET AT US.

AGREED.
AND THE OTHER PERSON...

...IS THE WAYNE FAMILY BUTLER, ALFRED. WHO OF COURSE IS NO LONGER WITH US...

THEN WHO...?

MY NAME IS THE OUTSIDER.
HUH?

MY NAME IS...

...THE OUTSIDER!

THE WAX DUMMIES!

THEY STOOD UP!

YOU TWO ARE GOING TO DIE!
YOU TWO ARE GOING TO DIE!
AND THEY'RE TALKING?!

BATMAN AND ROBIN!
YOU TWO ARE GOING TO DIE!

YOU'LL DIE 12 HOURS FROM NOW!
12 HOURS FROM NOW...

...

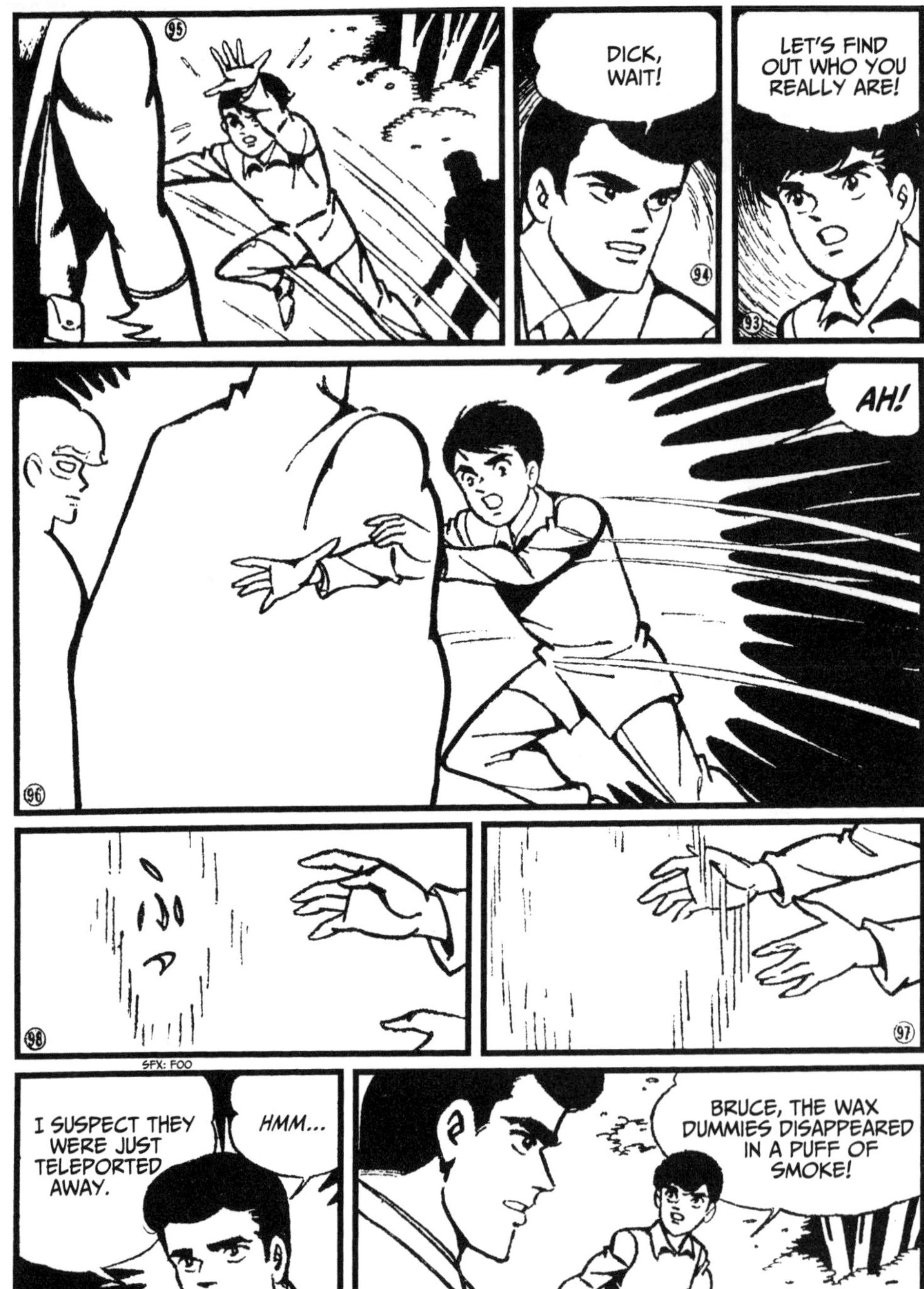
LET'S FIND OUT WHO YOU REALLY ARE!
DICK, WAIT!
AH!
SFX: FOO
BRUCE, THE WAX DUMMIES DISAPPEARED IN A PUFF OF SMOKE!
HMM...
I SUSPECT THEY WERE JUST TELEPORTED AWAY.

BATMAN! IF WE CATCH THE CREEPS THAT DELIVERED THE COFFINS, WE'LL PROBABLY GET SOME ANSWERS!
MM...
WE'LL PURSUE THEM IN THE BATMOBILE!
ALL RIGHT!

In a flash, the two changed into their heroic guises and roared out of the Batcave.

SFX: VROOOM

Batman drove the atomic-powered Batmobile as fast as it would go to chase that truck, little knowing that the Outsider's deadly trap was waiting for them!

SFX: VROOOM

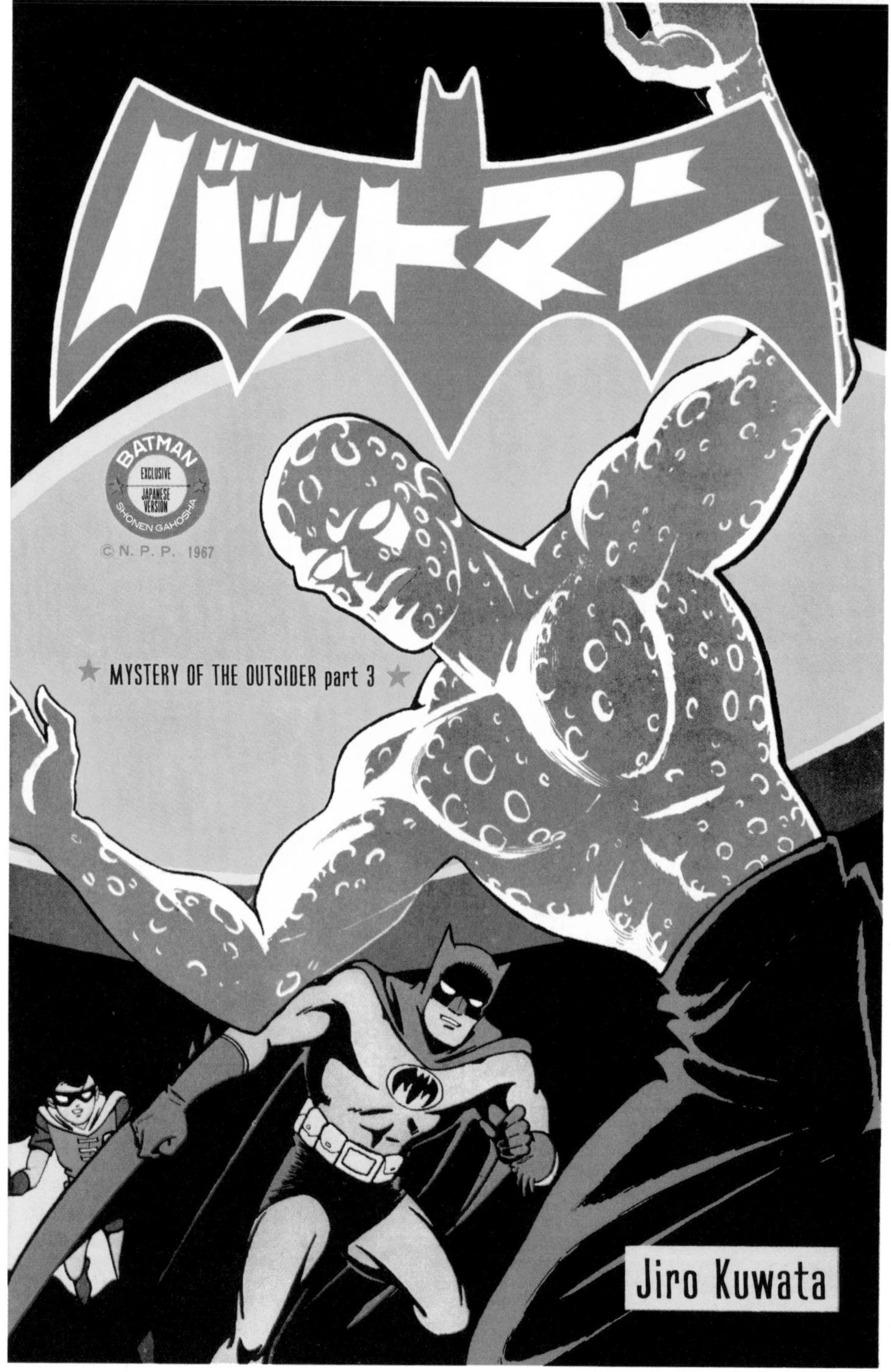
バットマン
BATMAN
EXCLUSIVE
JAPANESE VERSION
SHONEN GAHOSHA
©N. P. P. 1967
MYSTERY OF THE OUTSIDER part 3
Jiro Kuwata

LAST EPISODE...
Two coffins were delivered to Batman and Robin. Inside were two wax effigies of the Dynamic Duo. The dummies declared, "You two are going to die 12 hours from now," and then disappeared in a puff of smoke! Batman and Robin pursued the truck that dropped off the coffins.

SFX: WHOOSH

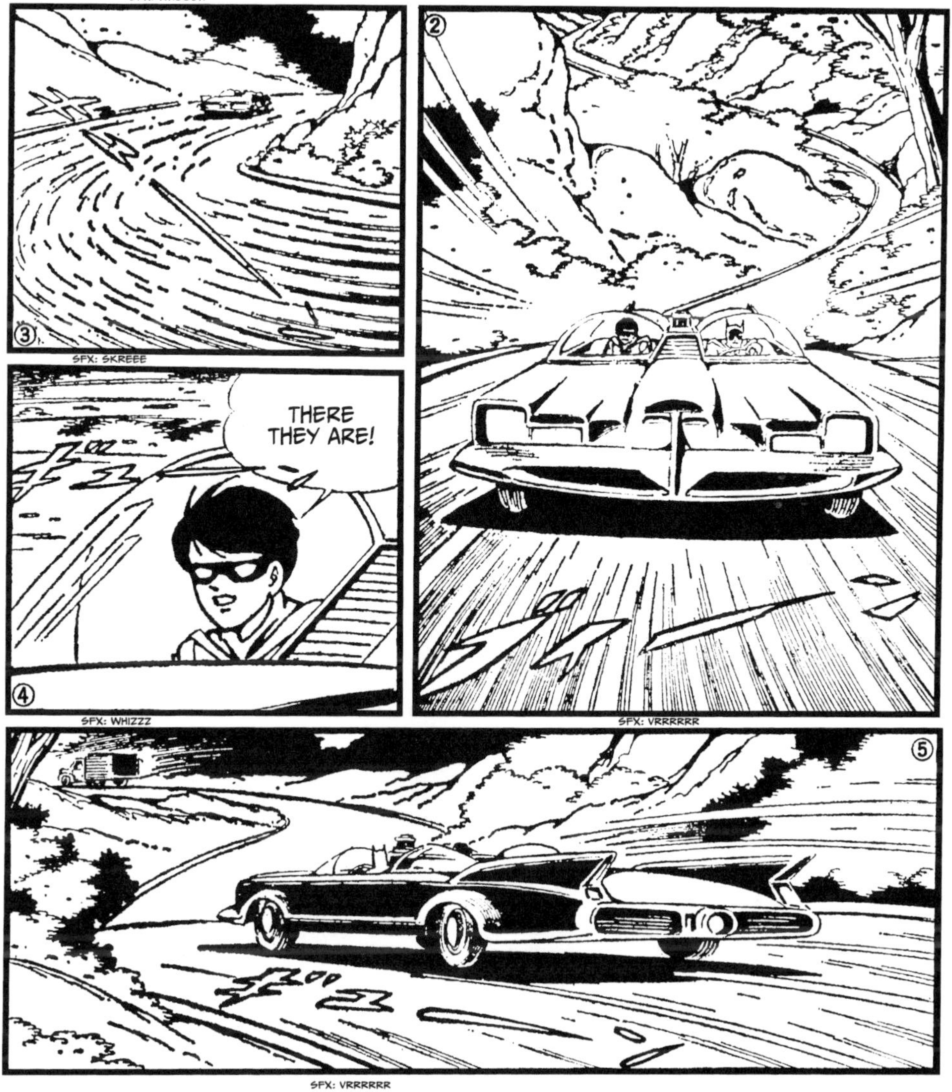

SFX: VRRRRRR

SFX: SKREEE

THERE THEY ARE!

SFX: WHIZZZ

SFX: VRRRRRR

SFX: VROOOO

PULL OVER! THERE'S SOMETHING WE WANT TO ASK YOU!

AAAH! STUPID TRUCK! IT RAMMED US!
SFX: VROOOO
SFX: SMASH

SFX: VRRRRR

WELL, THEY'RE OBVIOUSLY PUTTING UP A FIGHT!

ALL RIGHT, ROBIN! PREPARE A BAT-SMOKESCREEN!

GOTCHA! THEY'LL HAVE TO STOP WHETHER THEY LIKE IT OR NOT.

HERE WE GO!

SFX: VRRRRRR

SFX: SKREEE

THERE!

SFX: WHOOF

WELL, THEY'VE STOPPED. NOW DON'T LET THEM GET AWAY!

SFX: SWISH

AAAH! JUMPING OUT OF THE CAB...
WHO ARE THOSE MASKED MEN?!

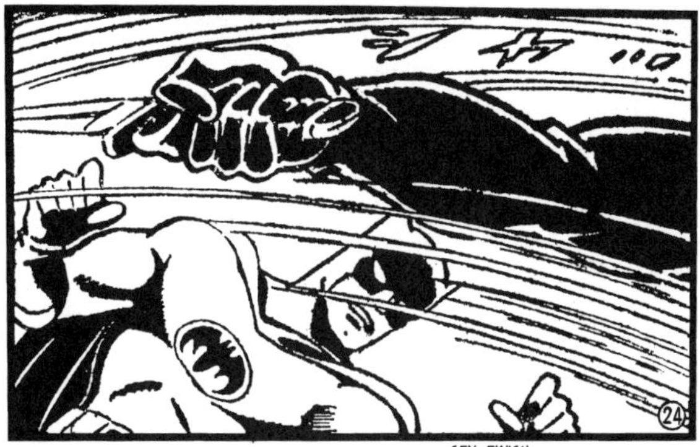
24

23

SFX: FWISH

26

SFX: KRAK

25

SFX: SLASH

28

27

SFX: BAM

29

SFX: TAP

SFX: HOP

SFX: SOK

B-BATMAN, NO MATTER HOW MANY TIMES YOU POUND THESE GUYS, THEY KEEP COMING AT YOU!

IT'S LIKE THEY'RE NOT EVEN HUMAN!
SFX: WHAK

SFX: WHUMP

SFX: HOP

SFX: TA TA TA TA

SFX: FREEZE

?

SFX: TA TA TA

SFX: FREEZE

?

NOW WHAT'S UP WITH THESE MASKED MANIACS?!

THEY'VE ALL SUDDENLY STOPPED MOVING...

SFX: WOBBLE

SFX: WHUMP

AH! ONE FELL OVER.

SFX: WOBBLE WOBBLE

THIS ONE, TOO!

SFX: BAM

THEY ALL FELL DOWN.
WHAT THE DEVIL IS THIS...?

BATMAN! THIS MAN'S DEAD!

THIS ONE, TOO...
THEY'RE ALL DEAD!

DID WE BEAT THEM TO DEATH?
WE WEREN'T THAT ROUGH.

STILL, HOW COULD THEY ALL SUDDENLY DIE LIKE THAT, AS IF ON CUE?
IT DOESN'T MAKE ANY SENSE...

ANYWAY, LET'S TURN THE BODIES OVER TO THE POLICE.
WE MAY GET SOME ANSWERS THERE.

ゴッタム警察署
SIGN: GOTHAM POLICE DEPARTMENT
BATMAN, I'M STUNNED. WHAT A BIZARRE CASE...

WE INVESTIGATED THOSE THREE MASKED MEN...

...AND ALL THREE WERE CRIMINALS WHO DIED RECENTLY AND WERE BURIED IN THE SAME CEMETERY.
WHAT?! THEY WERE ALREADY DEAD?!

SO DEAD MEN ROSE FROM THE GRAVE, DELIVERED WAX REPLICAS OF US...
...AND THEN ENGAGED US IN COMBAT?

UNBELIEVABLE AS IT IS, THAT'S WHAT HAPPENED.

HMM... IT SEEMS THIS OUTSIDER POSSESSES THE POWER TO ANIMATE THE DEAD!

COME TO THINK OF IT, EVEN THOSE WAX DUMMIES WALKED AND TALKED BEFORE DISAPPEARING.

COME ON, ROBIN! WE DON'T HAVE TIME TO CHEW THE FAT!
AND THAT WAS FIVE HOURS AGO.

AND ON TOP OF THAT, HE BOASTED OF MURDERING US "12 HOURS FROM NOW."

I DON'T THINK WE'RE DEALING WITH AN ORDINARY CRIMINAL HERE...
THE OUTSIDER...

GODSPEED, YOU TWO!
SFX: SLAM

WHERE ARE WE GOING?
FIRST, WE'LL CHECK OUT THE CEMETERY.

BATMAN, THE CEMETERY WHERE THOSE THREE CROOKS WERE BURIED IS IN THE OTHER DIRECTION...

SFX: VROOOO

WE'RE NOT GOING TO THAT CEMETERY, BUT THE ONE WITH THE WAYNE FAMILY CRYPT.

THE WAYNE FAMILY CRYPT?
WHY?

I WANT TO CHECK ON ALFRED'S BODY.

IF THE OUTSIDER CAN ANIMATE CORPSES, THEN IT BECOMES NECESSARY TO INVESTIGATE THE DEAD.

PLUS, OUR BUTLER ALFRED WAS THE ONLY PERSON...

...WHO KNEW OUR TRUE IDENTITIES.

MAYBE *HE'S* THE OUTSIDER...

OH, COME ON! THAT CAN'T BE...

I HOPE YOU'RE RIGHT...

ウェイン家墓地

SIGN: WAYNE FAMILY CRYPT

ALFRED SHOULD BE DOWN HERE SLEEPING PEACEFULLY FOR ETERNITY IN A REFRIGERATED COFFIN.
BUT IF ALFRED'S BODY ISN'T IN HERE, THEN HE'S DEFINITELY THE OUTSIDER.
I'LL OPEN IT.
GO AHEAD.
ALFRED!

GO AHEAD, CLOSE IT UP.

PHEW... HIS BODY IS DEFINITELY STILL LAID TO REST.

BUT NOW WE KNOW THAT ALFRED'S NOT THE OUTSIDER.

THE WHOLE IDEA IS SILLY! COME ON, ALFRED NEVER WOULD'VE TURNED AGAINST US.

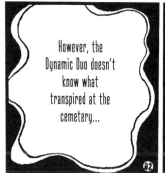

However, the Dynamic Duo doesn't know what transpired at the cemetery...

Crawford, a scientist, carried Alfred's corpse out of the crypt...

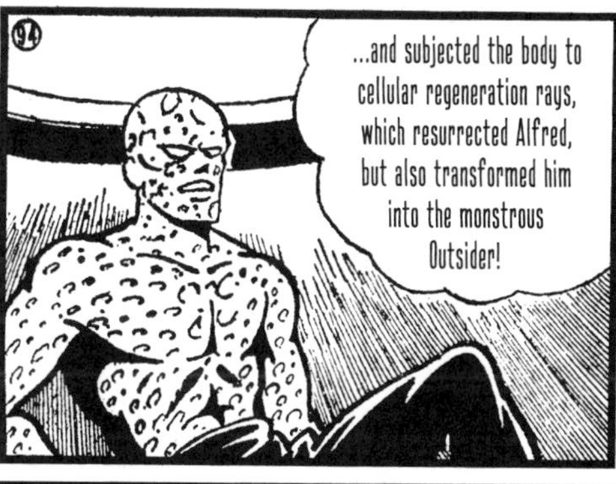
...and subjected the body to cellular regeneration rays, which resurrected Alfred, but also transformed him into the monstrous Outsider!

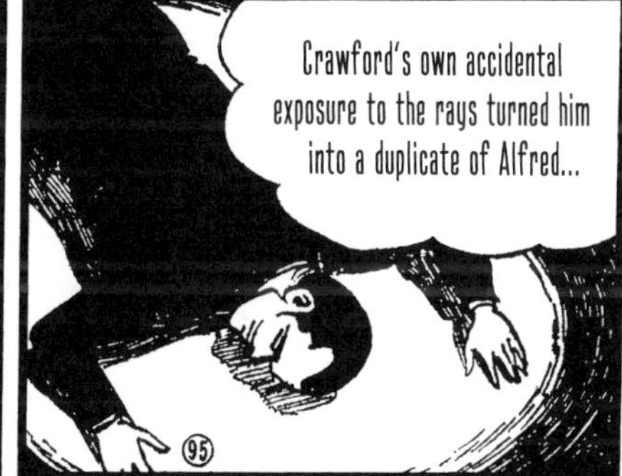
Crawford's own accidental exposure to the rays turned him into a duplicate of Alfred...

...and it's this duplicate that's in the refrigerated coffin in Alfred's stead.

BATMAN, TEN HOURS HAVE PASSED! DO YOU HAVE ANY CLUES?
WAIT!

I GOT A REACTION FROM ONE OF THE COFFINS!

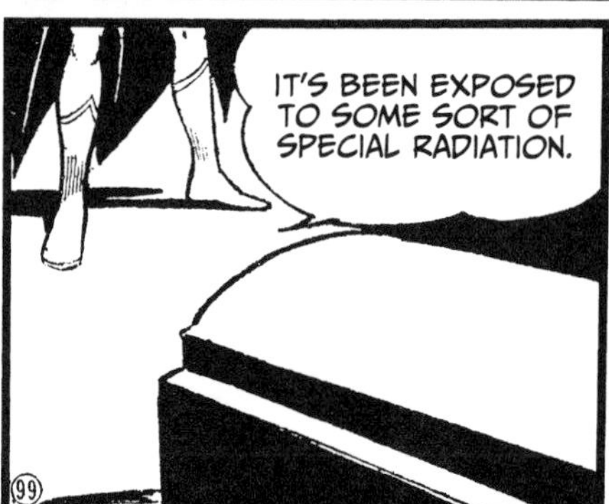
IT'S BEEN EXPOSED TO SOME SORT OF SPECIAL RADIATION.

ROBIN! CHECK OUT THE WAVELENGTH OF THE RADIATION!

ROGER!

SFX: BEEP BEEP BEEP

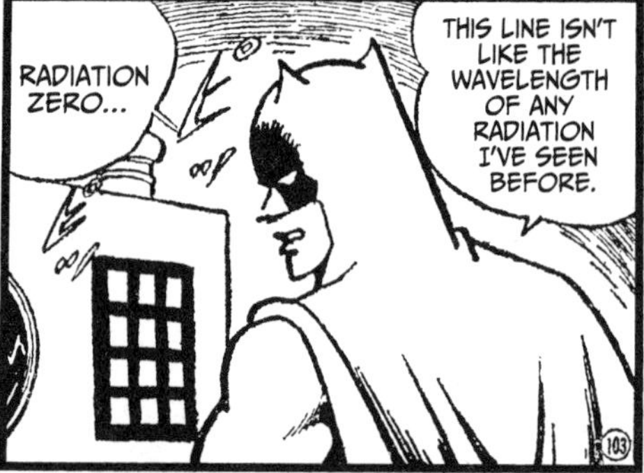
THIS LINE ISN'T LIKE THE WAVELENGTH OF ANY RADIATION I'VE SEEN BEFORE.
RADIATION ZERO...

SFX: BEEP BEEP

OKAY, ROBIN, LET'S SET THE TRACKER IN THE BATMOBILE TO THIS RADIATION ZERO.

NOW, LET'S GO! THE RADIATION DETECTOR WILL LEAD US TO THE LOCATION THAT'S GIVING OFF RADIATION ZERO!

THAT'S WHERE WE'LL FIND THE OUTSIDER.

Mean-while...

⚟CHUCKLE⚞ THE MATTER TRANSFORMER HAS STARTED TO WORK. ALREADY, 11 HOURS HAVE PASSED!
SFX: BEEP BEEP

ONE MORE HOUR TO GO!
IF I DON'T STOP THIS MACHINE WITHIN THE NEXT HOUR...

...BETWEEN THE MATTER TRANSFORMER AND MY PSYCHOKINESIS, BATMAN AND ROBIN WILL DIE BY MELTING INTO PUDDLES OF GOO!

バットマン
★MYSTERY OF THE OUTSIDER part 4★
BATMAN
EXCLUSIVE
JAPANESE VERSION
SHONEN GAHOSHA
©N. P. P. 1967
Jiro Kuwata

SFX: VROOO

LAST EPISODE...

The Outsider has set an invisible trap for Batman and Robin. Eleven hours have passed since he turned on the matter transformation device. Unless the machine is turned off within the hour, the Dynamic Duo will die by melting into a not-so-dynamic puddle. Meanwhile, Batman and Robin are tracking down The Outsider by using the Batmobile's tracking device to pick up traces of the unusual radiation the villain left in the coffins that he had delivered to them!

RADIATION ZERO IS COMING FROM WITHIN THIS MANSION.

I BET IT'S THE OUTSIDER'S HIDEOUT...
I'D TAKE THAT BET.

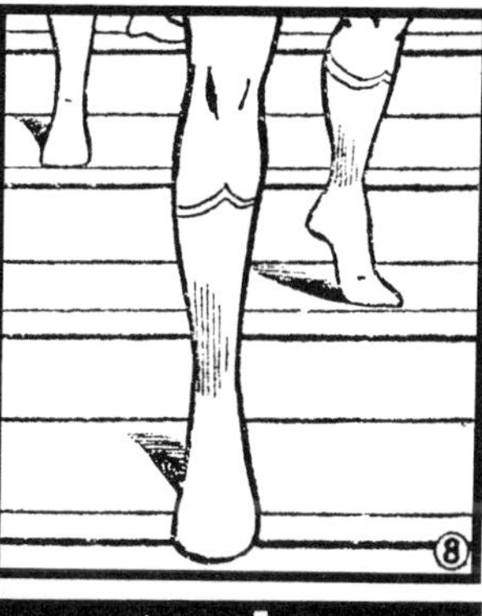

SFX: CREAK

WELL... THIS IS AN IMPRESSIVE LAB.

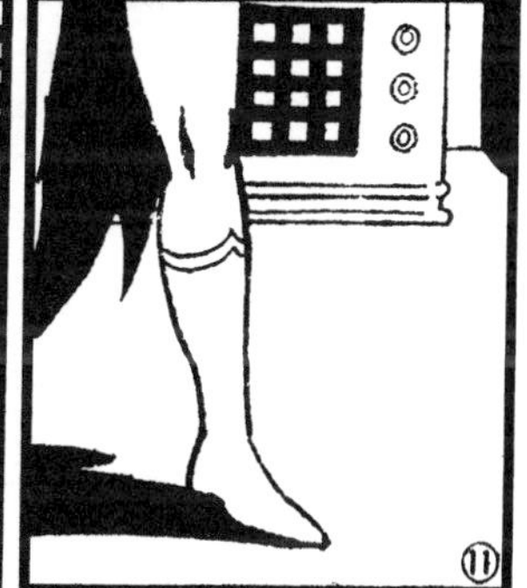

SFX: SHUDDER

SFX: SHUDDER

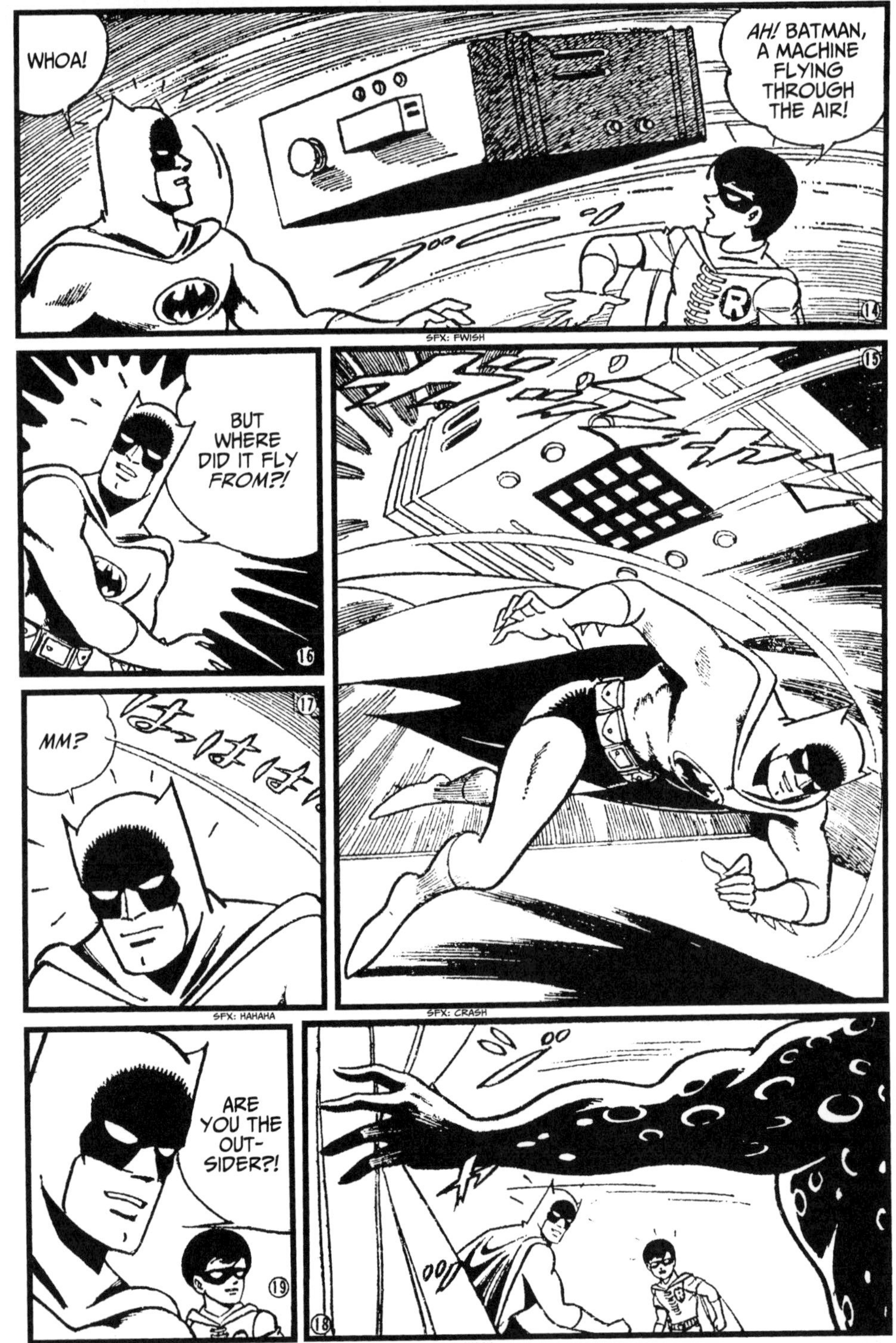
WHOA!
AH! BATMAN, A MACHINE FLYING THROUGH THE AIR!
SFX: FWISH
SFX: CRASH
BUT WHERE DID IT FLY FROM?!
MM?
SFX: HAHAHA
SFX: SWISH
ARE YOU THE OUT-SIDER?!

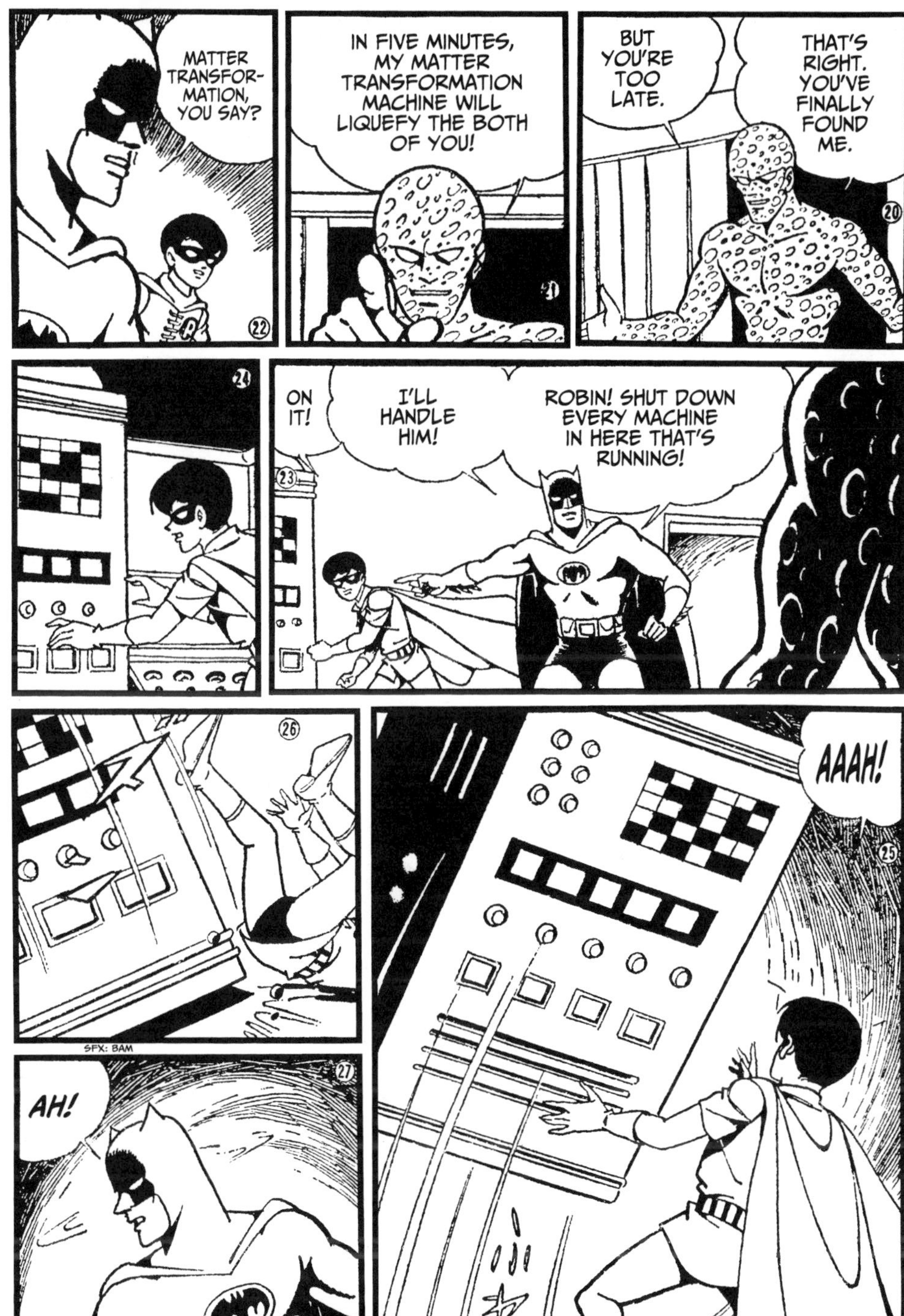
THAT'S RIGHT. YOU'VE FINALLY FOUND ME.
BUT YOU'RE TOO LATE.
IN FIVE MINUTES, MY MATTER TRANSFORMATION MACHINE WILL LIQUEFY THE BOTH OF YOU!
MATTER TRANSFOR-MATION, YOU SAY?
ROBIN! SHUT DOWN EVERY MACHINE IN HERE THAT'S RUNNING!
I'LL HANDLE HIM!
ON IT!
AAAH!
SFX: SWISH
SFX: BAM
AH!

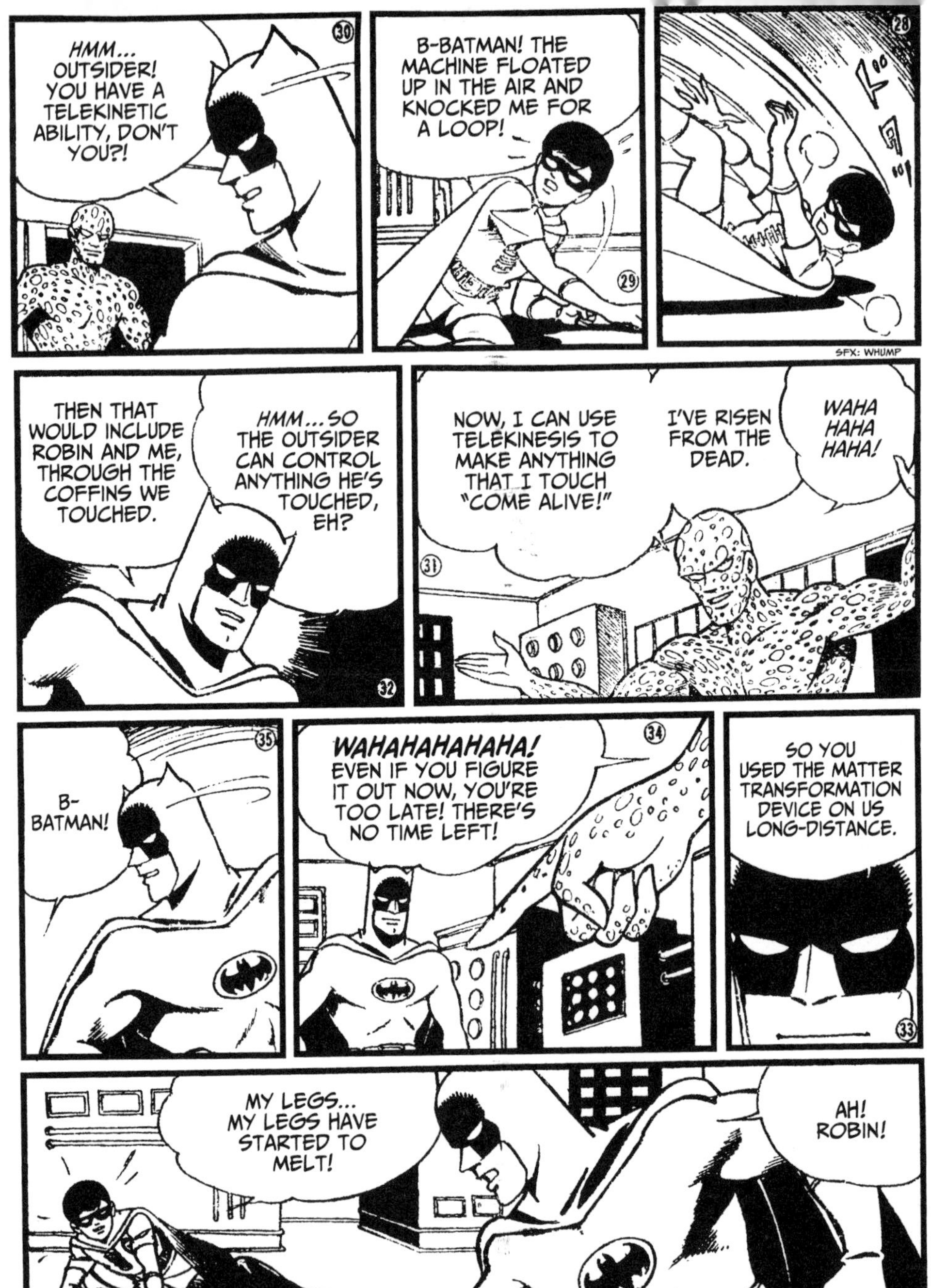
SFX: WHUMP
B-BATMAN! THE MACHINE FLOATED UP IN THE AIR AND KNOCKED ME FOR A LOOP!
HMM... OUTSIDER! YOU HAVE A TELEKINETIC ABILITY, DON'T YOU?!
WAHA HAHA HAHA!
I'VE RISEN FROM THE DEAD.
NOW, I CAN USE TELEKINESIS TO MAKE ANYTHING THAT I TOUCH "COME ALIVE!"
HMM...SO THE OUTSIDER CAN CONTROL ANYTHING HE'S TOUCHED, EH?
THEN THAT WOULD INCLUDE ROBIN AND ME, THROUGH THE COFFINS WE TOUCHED.
SO YOU USED THE MATTER TRANSFORMATION DEVICE ON US LONG-DISTANCE.
WAHAHAHAHAHA! EVEN IF YOU FIGURE IT OUT NOW, YOU'RE TOO LATE! THERE'S NO TIME LEFT!
B- BATMAN!
AH! ROBIN!
MY LEGS... MY LEGS HAVE STARTED TO MELT!

AT LONG LAST, YOU TWO ARE MEETING YOUR END! HOW DOES IT FEEL?!
WAHA HAHA HAHA!

DARN IT! I CAN'T EVEN STAND UP!

THAT'S RIGHT. I TOUCHED THE COFFIN 30 SECONDS AFTER ROBIN.

SO I HAVE 30 SECONDS LEFT!

SFX: SWISH

SFX: CRASH CRASH CRASH

SFX: KRAK

SFX: WHUMP

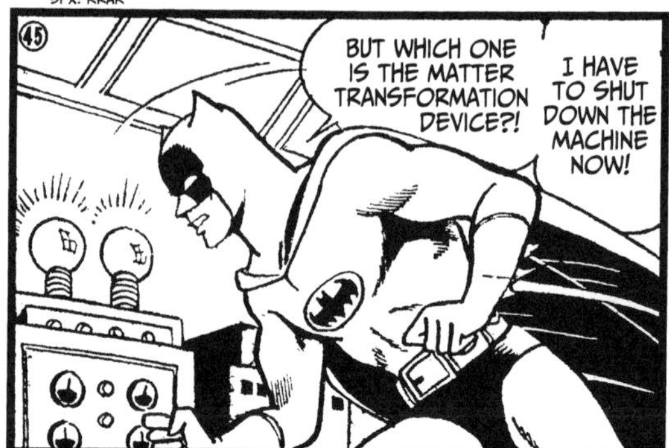
BUT WHICH ONE IS THE MATTER TRANSFORMATION DEVICE?!
I HAVE TO SHUT DOWN THE MACHINE NOW!

SFX: BEEP BEEP

THERE ARE TWO LAMPS! THAT HAS TO BE IT!

SFX: SWISH

SFX: WHOOSH

SFX: GRAB

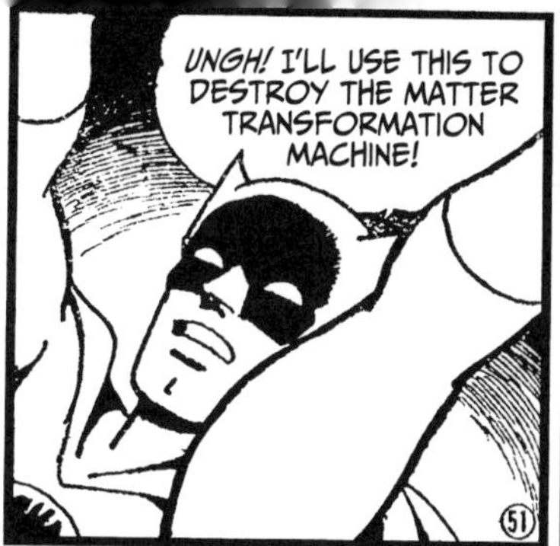
UNGH! I'LL USE THIS TO DESTROY THE MATTER TRANSFORMATION MACHINE!

SFX: SMASH

SFX: BOOM

AH! MY LEGS ARE COMING BACK!

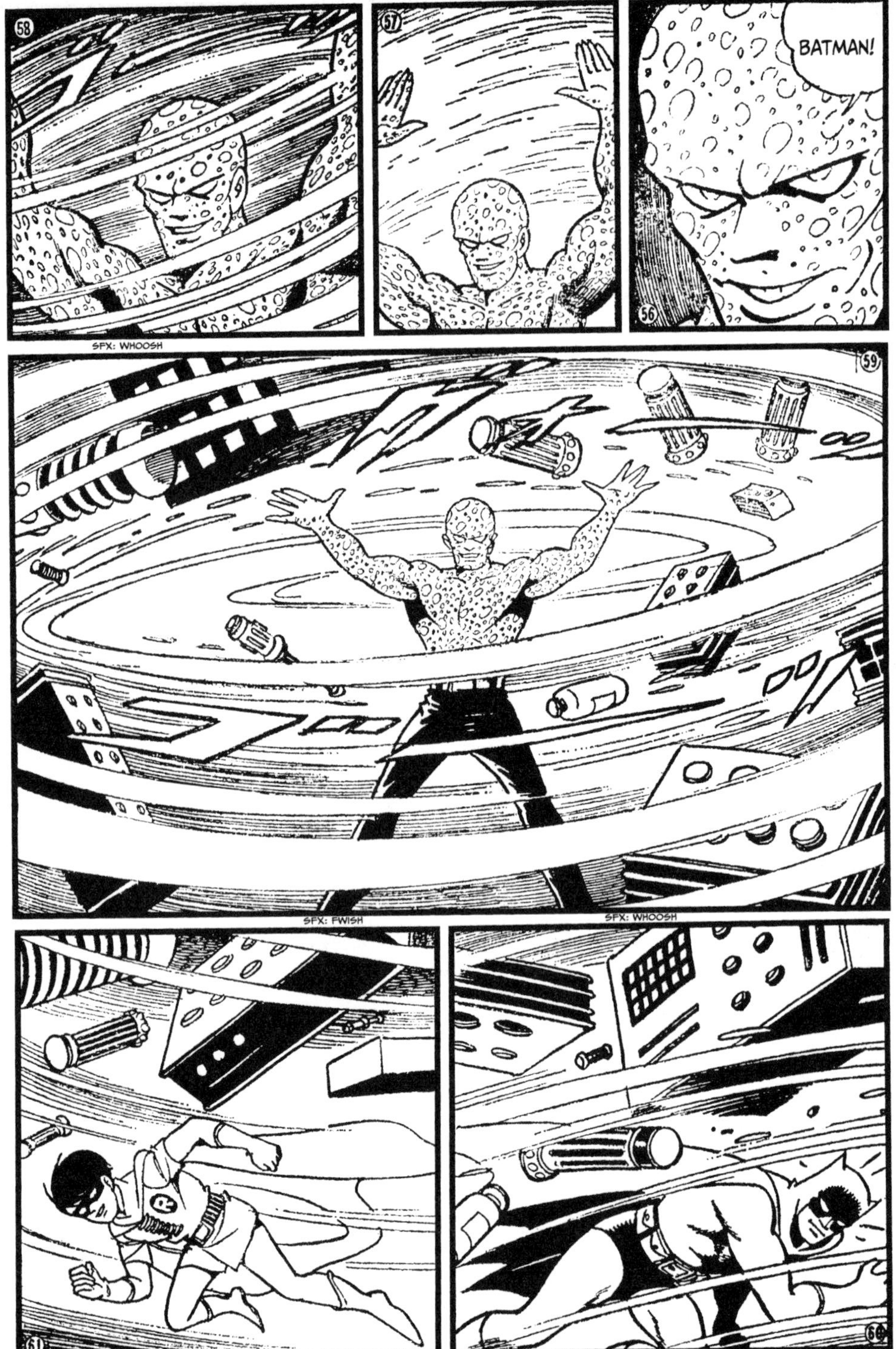
BATMAN!
SFX: WHOOSH
SFX: WHOOSH
SFX: FWISH

SFX: WHIZZZ
AH!
SFX: CLUNK
SFX: HUMMM
SFX: HUMMM

AAAH! YOU KNOCKED ME INTO THE LEVER OF THE CELLULAR REGENERATION DEVICE!
SFX: HUMMM
SFX: HUMMM
AAAAH!
B-BATMAN! THE OUTSIDER'S FORM IS CHANGING...

SFX: SLUMP

ALFRED!

MMM...

ROBIN! PULL THE LEVER!

SFX: CLANK

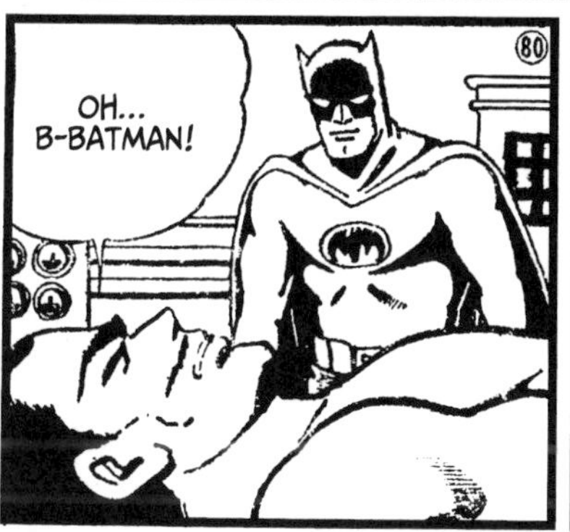
OH... B-BATMAN!

WHAT WAS I DOING? *EH...?* I FEEL LIKE I JUST HAD THE MOST FRIGHTFUL DREAM.
...

THAT'S RIGHT, OLD FRIEND. YOU WERE HAVING A BAD DREAM.

ALFRED HAS NO MEMORY OF BEING THE OUTSIDER!
MM. AND THERE'S NO REASON TO REMIND HIM EITHER.

THIS HAPPENED BECAUSE HIS SINGLE-MINDED DESIRE TO SAVE US WAS PERVERTED BY A MALFUNCTIONING RAY.

SFX: VRRRR

LET'S TAKE ALFRED HOME, ROBIN. THEN THERE'S SOMEWHERE I HAVE TO GO.

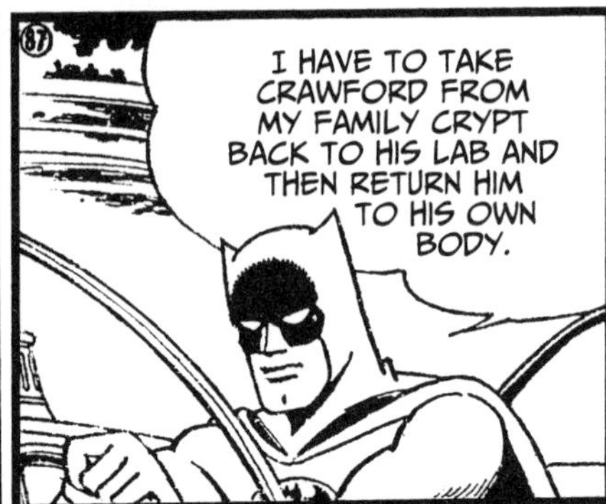
I HAVE TO TAKE CRAWFORD FROM MY FAMILY CRYPT BACK TO HIS LAB AND THEN RETURN HIM TO HIS OWN BODY.

ウエイン家墓地

SIGN: WAYNE FAMILY CRYPT

After getting Alfred home safely, Batman retrieved Crawford's body from the Wayne family crypt, took him back to his lab, and exposed him to the cellular regeneration rays once more.

HELLO, CRAWFORD. WELCOME BACK TO THE LAND OF THE LIVING.

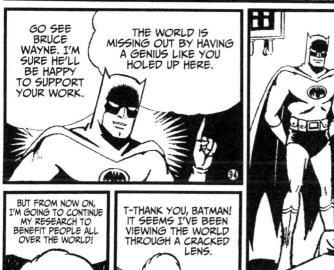

THE WORLD IS MISSING OUT BY HAVING A GENIUS LIKE YOU HOLED UP HERE.
GO SEE BRUCE WAYNE. I'M SURE HE'LL BE HAPPY TO SUPPORT YOUR WORK.

T-THANK YOU, BATMAN! IT SEEMS I'VE BEEN VIEWING THE WORLD THROUGH A CRACKED LENS.
BUT FROM NOW ON, I'M GOING TO CONTINUE MY RESEARCH TO BENEFIT PEOPLE ALL OVER THE WORLD!

Eventually, Alfred made a full recovery...

AHHH! WHAT A BEAUTIFUL MORNING!

MASTER DICK, BREAKFAST IS READY.
THANK YOU, ALFRED.

MORNING, DICK! HAVE A SEAT. I ALREADY STARTED WITHOUT YOU.

THINGS SURE ARE MORE FUN AROUND HERE WHEN WE'VE GOT ALFRED.
YOU CAN SAY THAT AGAIN...

ドカーン
AAAH!

SFX: BOOM

W-WHAT HAPPENED?!

OH, BOY... ANOTHER ONE OF CRAWFORD'S EXPERIMENTS WENT UP IN SMOKE...

Jiro Kuwata
BRUCE! BRUCE!
WHAT IS IT, DICK?
APPARENTLY, THERE'S BEEN ANOTHER SIGHTING OF THE MONSTER OF GORE BAY!

バットマ
★ THE MONSTER OF GORE BAY ★
BATMAN
EXCLUSIVE
JAPANESE VERSION
SHONEN GAHOSHA
©N. P. P. 1967
④
OH...
THE PAPER SAYS THE BEAST FIRST REARED ITS HEAD IN THE BAY ABOUT SIX MONTHS AGO.
⑤
GUESS A LOT OF PEOPLE HAVE BEEN GATHERING AT THE BAY TO TRY TO SPOT THE MONSTER THEMSELVES.
I SEE...

怪獣またもゴア湾にあらわる!!
HEADLINE: MONSTER APPEARS AGAIN IN GORE BAY!

THERE'S EVEN A PHOTO AND EVERYTHING. PERHAPS IT'S NOT A HOAX.

OF COURSE IT'S NOT A HOAX!

SAY, WHY DON'T WE TAKE A NIGHT OFF AND TRY TO GET A GLIMPSE OF THE CREATURE OURSELVES?
CERTAINLY NOT.

PROTECTING GOTHAM CITY IS OUR SACRED DUTY.

ONE ITEM ON OUR AGENDA IS FINDING PROFESSOR CAHN, WHO WAS KIDNAPPED BY PERSON OR PERSONS UNKNOWN ABOUT A MONTH AGO.
カーン博士
TEXT: PROFESSOR CAHN

AND WE HAVEN'T CAUGHT SPENCE AND HIS GANG YET, WHO GOT AWAY CLEAN AFTER ROBBING GOTHAM BANK OF A HEFTY SUM.
スペンス
TEXT: SPENCE

THIS IS NO TIME TO GO MONSTER WATCHING.
SHUCKS...

WELL, TIME TO GO OUT ON PATROL, CHUM.

A REAL MONSTER...

I REALLY WANTED TO SEE IT...

HEY, ROBIN, YOUR SUIT'S ON BACKWARDS!

WAIT A SECOND! THAT'S *MY* CAPE!

FOCUS! IT'S LIKE YOU'VE GOT MONSTERS ON THE BRAIN!

SFX: SHOVE

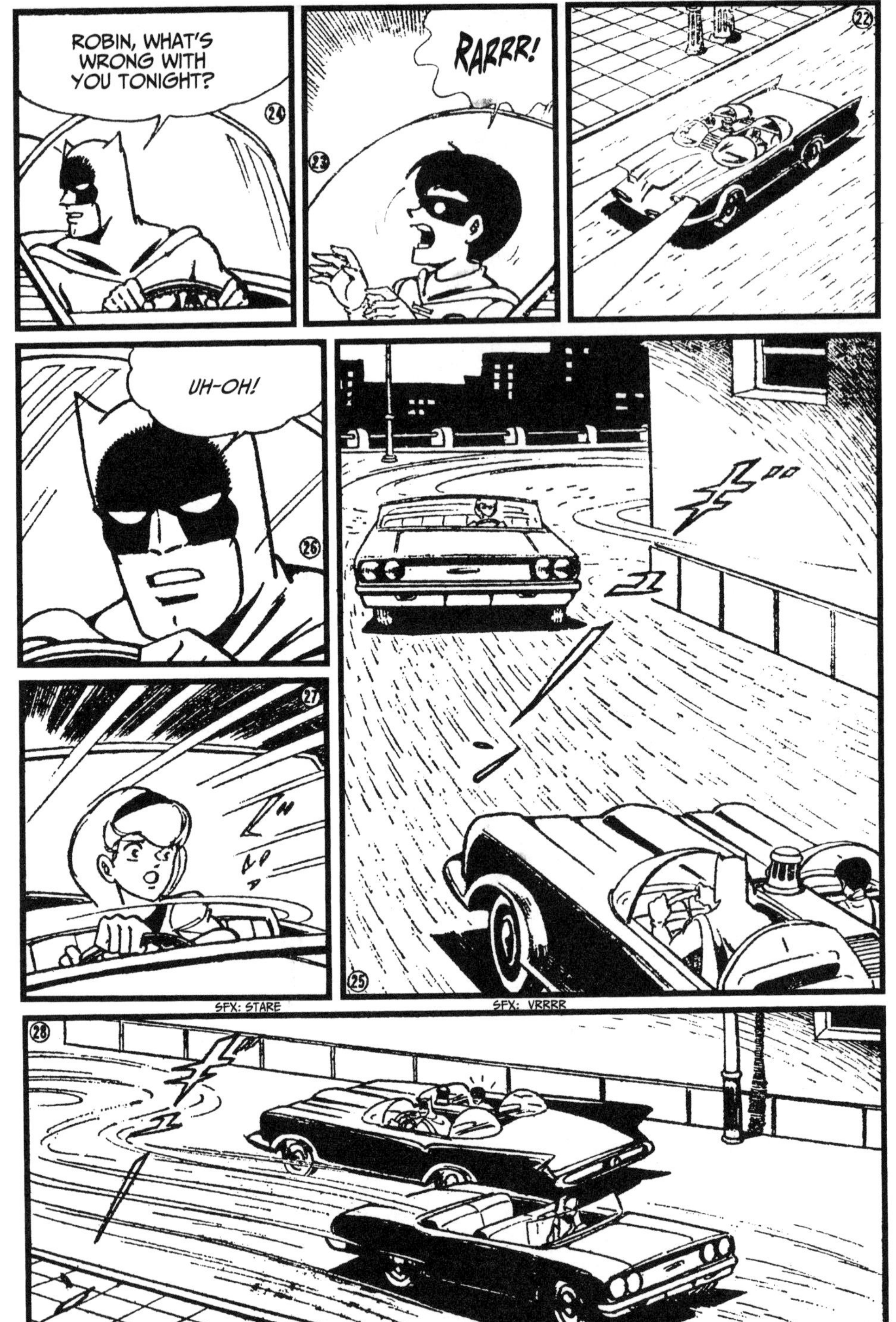
RARRR!
ROBIN, WHAT'S WRONG WITH YOU TONIGHT?
SFX: VRRRR
UH-OH!
SFX: STARE

SFX: ZOOM

SFX: CRASH

S-SHE CRASHED!

OOOH...
MISS, ARE YOU OKAY?!

I DON'T HAVE TIME TO BE IN PAIN RIGHT NOW!

SFX: FWISH

OWWW...

OH, BATMAN!
HUH? AREN'T YOU HELEN, THE DAUGHTER OF THE MISSING PROFESSOR CAHN?

COME ON, HOP IN THE BATMOBILE.
WE'LL TAKE YOU TO THE HOSPITAL.

THERE'S NO TIME FOR THAT! I WAS JUST ON MY WAY TO THE POLICE...
SO RUNNING INTO YOU LIKE THIS IS PERFECT TIMING, BATMAN.

TAKE A LOOK AT THIS! IT'S A LETTER FROM MY FATHER.
WHAT? FROM PROFESSOR CAHN?

THE SPENCE GANG IS HOLDING ME AT THEIR HIDEOUT.
THE MAP BELOW SHOWS ITS LOCATION. CONTACT THE POLICE AND HELP ME.
--CAHN

SO THE SPENCE GANG KIDNAPPED PROFESSOR CAHN!

HE MUST'VE WAITED FOR JUST THE RIGHT TIME TO SLIP A LETTER OUT...

ALL RIGHT! LET'S GO, ROBIN!

HELEN! WAIT WITH CHIEF GORDON AT THE POLICE STATION!
WE'LL BE BACK SOON WITH PROFESSOR CAHN!

SFX: VROOOO

HANG A LEFT AT THE NEXT CORNER!

SFX: SKREEE
THIS IS IT!
HUH? THE DOOR'S NOT LOCKED...
SFX: CREAK
WHY, THERE'S NO ONE HERE...
I THINK IT'S ABAN-DONED.

LOOK AT ALL THE DUST THAT'S ACCUMULATED.
WHOEVER WAS HERE MOVED SOME TIME AGO.

BUT HELEN JUST GOT THAT LETTER.

MY GUESS IS THAT PROFESSOR CAHN MANAGED TO THROW THE LETTER OUTSIDE A WINDOW WHEN HIS CAPTORS WEREN'T LOOKING, BUT IT MIGHT'VE TAKEN SEVERAL DAYS BEFORE A PASSERBY PICKED IT UP AND PUT IT IN A MAILBOX.

HUH? JUST ONE OVERTURNED CHAIR...

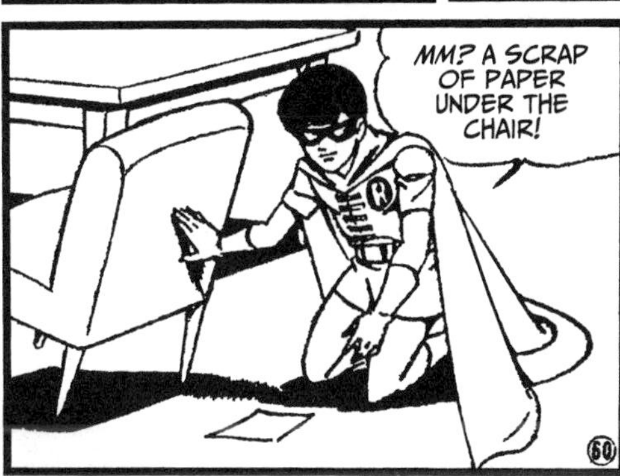
MM? A SCRAP OF PAPER UNDER THE CHAIR!

THERE'S WRITING ON IT...

ゴア湾怪獣

WRITING: MONSTER OF GORE BAY

MONSTER OF GORE BAY...

BATMAN, LOOK AT THIS. IT'S THE SAME HANDWRITING AS PROFESSOR CAHN'S LETTER.
HMM...

WHEN THEY MOVED CAHN OUT OF HERE, HE MUST'VE LEFT THIS BEHIND AS A CLUE.

IF THAT'S THE CASE, THEY TOOK HIM TO GORE BAY?!

ゴッタム
警察署
SIGN: GOTHAM POLICE STATION

WHAT?
MY FATHER'S BEEN TAKEN TO GORE BAY?

I CAN'T SAY FOR SURE.
BUT THAT'S WHAT THIS NOTE SEEMS TO INDICATE.
WELL, I TRUST YOUR INSTINCTS, BATMAN.

I'LL GO TO GORE BAY!

THE SPENCE GANG HAS HIM. A GIRL ON HER OWN WOULD BE HELPLESS AGAINST THEM.

I DON'T CARE WHO THEY ARE. SOMEHOW OR OTHER, I'LL GET MY FATHER BACK...

HOLD ON. I HAVE A FRIEND, BRUCE WAYNE.
I KNOW ABOUT HIM. THAT IS, IF YOU'RE REFERRING TO THE MILLIONAIRE.

YES, THAT'S THE ONE. AND I HEARD HE'S GOING TO GORE BAY.
HELEN, YOU SHOULD GO WITH HIM!

BATMAN! I'M... I MEAN, HIS WARD, DICK, IS GOING TOO, ISN'T HE?
YES. I SUPPOSE HE IS...
YAHOO!
?
HELLO, HELEN. SORRY TO KEEP YOU WAITING. I'M BRUCE WAYNE.
AND I'M RO... I MEAN, DICK.
NICE TO MEET YOU.

EVERYTHING'S READY FOR OUR DEPARTURE, SO WITHOUT FURTHER ADO...

WOW, WE'RE GOING BY PRIVATE PLANE? IMPRESSIVE!

SO I'LL FINALLY GET TO SEE THE MONSTER...

I DON'T CARE ABOUT ANY MONSTER, DICK.

OUR GOAL IS TO RESCUE PROFESSOR CAHN AND CAPTURE THE SPENCE GANG.

SFX: FWOOO

SFX: WHOOOSH

SFX: FWOOO

SFX: FWOOOO

SNORE
SNORE

HOW LONG ARE YOU PLANNING TO SLEEP, DICK? GORE BAY IS RIGHT BELOW US.
HUH?

WOW! WE'RE THERE ALREADY?!

SFX: FWOOO

SFX: FSSS FSSS FSSS FSSS

WHERE'S THE MONSTER?

YOU'RE BEING SILLY. IT'S NOT LIKE THE MONSTER IS ALWAYS AROUND.

BRUCE! WHAT'S THAT SHADOW BELOW?

OH! THE MONSTER OF GORE BAY!
IT'S RIGHT UNDER US!

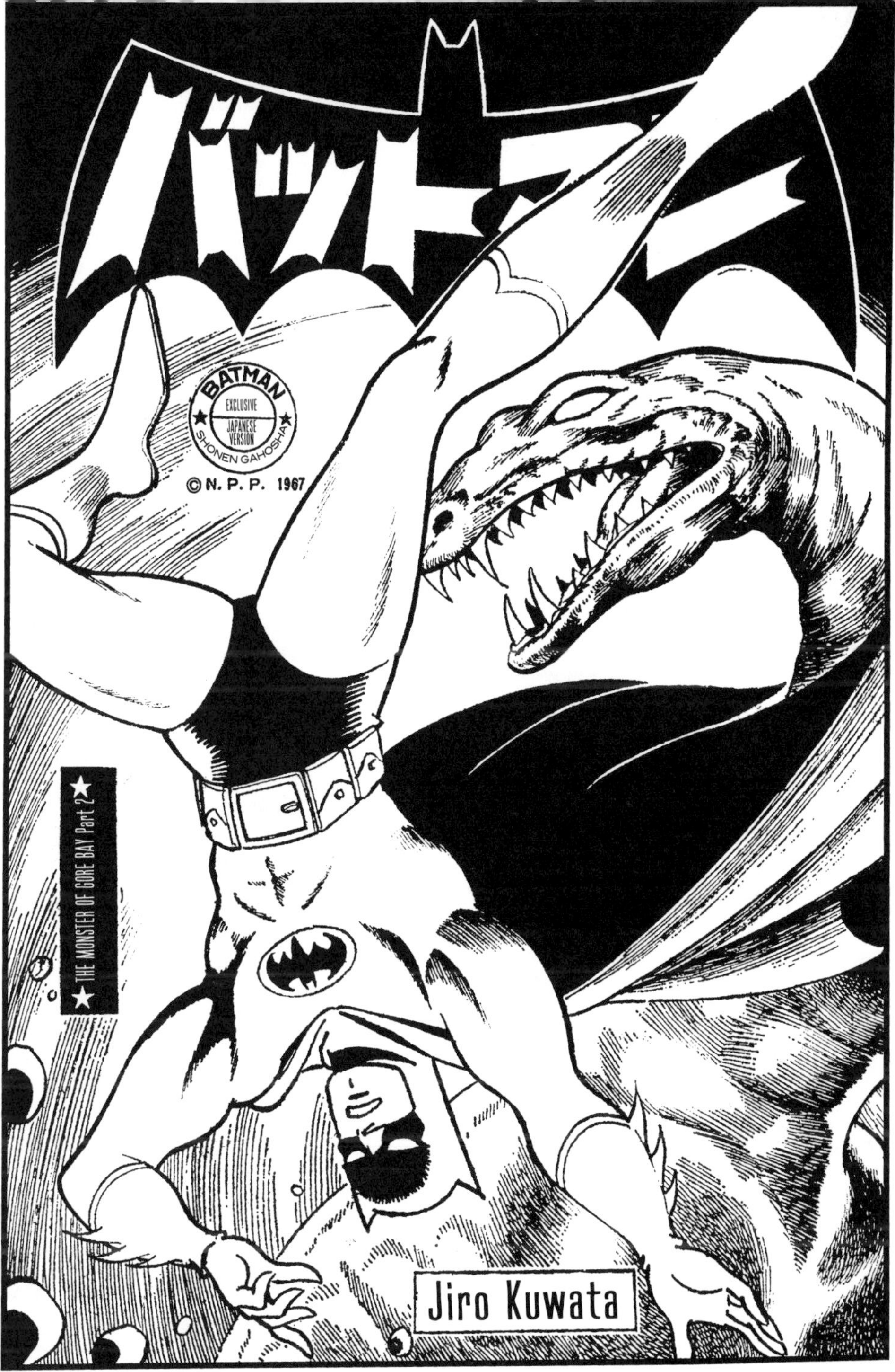

バットマン
BATMAN
EXCLUSIVE JAPANESE VERSION
SHONEN GAHOSHA
©N. P. P. 1967
★THE MONSTER OF GORE BAY Part 2★
Jiro Kuwata

LAST EPISODE...
In order to rescue Professor Cahn from the vicious Spence gang, Batman and Robin head for Gore Bay with Cahn's daughter, Helen. Gore Bay is abuzz with reports over a mysterious monster that appears from time to time. When the Caped Crusaders make a water landing in their airplane, a gigantic shadow rises up from the depths directly below them. It's the monster of Gore Bay!

GREAT SCOTT! LET'S GET AIRBORNE AGAIN!

AIEEE!

SFX:RARRR

SFX: BRRRR

SFX: SPLASH

SFX: FSSSSSHHH

SFX: SPLASH

PHEW! THAT WAS CLOSE. ONE SECOND LATER AND THE PLANE WOULD'VE BEEN CRUSHED.

WHERE'S THE MONSTER?

AAAH! OH, NO! IT'S HEADING TOWARDS THE SHORE!

IMAGINE THE HAVOC IT'LL WREAK IF IT MAKES IT TO LAND!

ALL RIGHT, LET'S LAND ON THE BEACH!

SFX: RRRRRR

SFX: CHFFFFF

COME ON, DICK! LET'S FIGHT THE BEAST IN OUR BATMAN AND ROBIN GUISES!

HELEN! TAKE SHELTER IN TOWN!

BATMAN! THE MONSTER'S MADE LANDFALL!

RIGHT!

AAAH! THE MONSTER'S COMING ASHORE!

SFX: SPLASH

RARRR!

SFX: CRASH

RUN! THE MONSTER'S ATTACKING!
IT CRUSHED A BEACH HUT!

SFX: VROOO

SFX: VROOO

HEY, IT'S BATMAN!
BATMAN AND ROBIN ARE HERE!

EVERYONE, TAKE COVER QUICKLY!
WE'LL DEAL WITH THE MONSTER!

LET'S GO, ROBIN!
OKAY!

THERE IT IS! DON'T SHOOT 'TIL WE GET UP CLOSE!

NOW! FIRE!

SFX: BLAM BLAM

SFX: THUK THUK

SFX: THUD THUD THUD
SFX: VRRR
KEEP SHOOTING WHILE I DRIVE RINGS AROUND IT!
GOTCHA!
SFX: BLAM BLAM BLAM
AAAR!
SFX: THUK
SFX: WHIZZZ
SFX: WHUD

AAAH!

NOT PART OF THE PLAN!

SFX: WHUD

SFX: WHUMP

SFX: THUD

SFX: GLARE

OKAY, LET'S SEE HOW IT LIKES A FIREBALL!

SFX: FWISH

SFX: FOOSH

WHA...?! THE BEAST IS BURNING UP!

SFX: SPLASH SPLASH SPLASH

SFX: FSSSS
SFX: BLUP BLUP BLUP

YAY! BATMAN DROVE THE MONSTER AWAY!

STRANGE... WHY WOULD THE CREATURE CATCH FIRE LIKE THAT?

OH, NO! SOMEBODY'S IN THE HUT THAT THE MONSTER CRUSHED!
WHAT?!

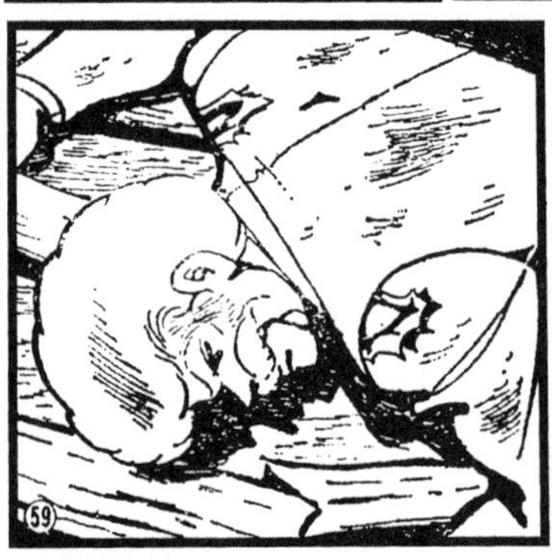

AH! IT'S PROFESSOR CAHN!

PAPA!

PAPA! SPEAK TO ME! PAPA!
IT'S OKAY! HE'S NOT DEAD. BUT WE'VE GOT TO GET HIM TO A HOSPITAL RIGHT AWAY.

病院
SIGN: HOSPITAL

WHAT'S THE PROGNOSIS, DOCTOR? WILL PROFESSOR CAHN MAKE IT?

I DON'T BELIEVE HIS LIFE IS IN DANGER.

BUT IT MAY BE A WHILE BEFORE HE'S ABLE TO SPEAK AGAIN.

IT'S FISHY ANY WAY YOU LOOK AT IT. IF PROFESSOR CAHN WAS A CAPTIVE OF THE SPENCE GANG, WHAT WAS HE DOING IN A HUT ON THE BEACH?

WELL, THEY PROBABLY SHUT HIM UP INSIDE THERE, RIGHT?

BUT THERE WAS NO TRACE OF THE SPENCE GANG.

AIEEE!
AH!

THAT'S HELEN SCREAMING!

SFX: SWISH

W-WHAT'S WRONG?!
T-THAT! THAT...

AH! A DAGGER EMBEDDED IN PROFESSOR CAHN'S BED!

SOMEONE THREW IT IN FROM THAT WINDOW!

OVER THERE!
HALT!
SFX: FWISH
ULP!
AAAH!
SFX: WHAM

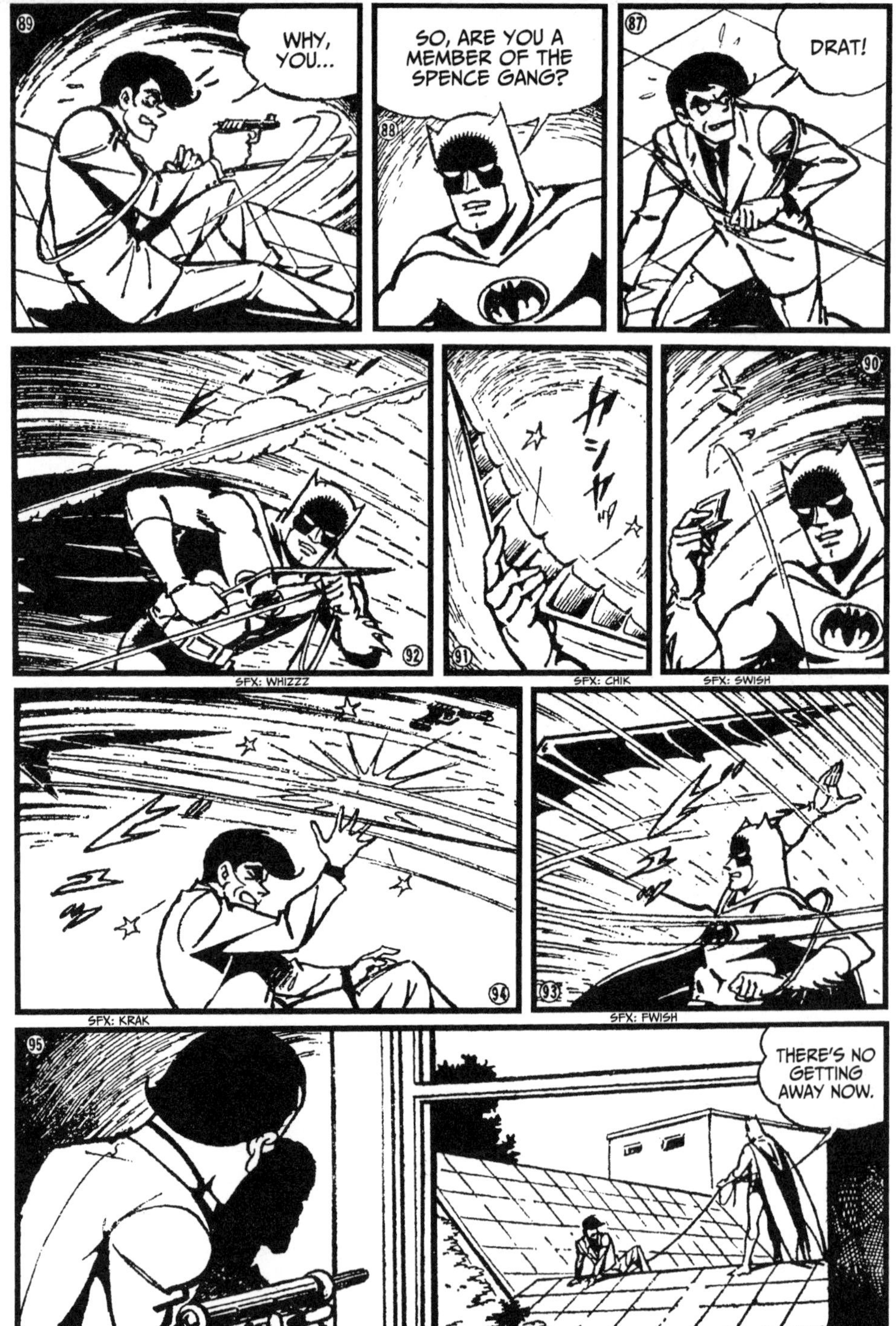
DRAT!
SO, ARE YOU A MEMBER OF THE SPENCE GANG?
WHY, YOU...
SFX: SWISH
SFX: CHIK
SFX: WHIZZZ
SFX: FWISH
SFX: KRAK
THERE'S NO GETTING AWAY NOW.

SO TALK! THE FIRST THING I WANT TO KNOW IS WHY YOU TRIED TO FINISH OFF THE GRAVELY WOUNDED PROFESSOR CAHN!
SFX: BUDDA-BUDDA-BUDDA
SFX: BUDDA-BUDDA-BUDDA
WAHAHAHA! THAT'S WHAT YOU GET!

LAST EPISODE...

A gravely wounded victim was found under the beach hut that was crushed by the monster of Gore Bay. His identity was none other than Prof. Cahn, who was supposedly being held captive by the Spence gang. That same day, while Cahn was being treated at a hospital, a dagger was thrown into his room. Batman took off after the assailant, but suddenly, a torrent of machine gun fire from the window of another building was headed straight for the Caped Crusader!

バットマ

★ THE MONSTER OF GORE BAY Part 3 ★

BATMAN EXCLUSIVE JAPANESE VERSION SHONEN GAHOSHA

Jiro Kuwata

②
SFX: SWISH

③
SFX: CHAK

④

AH! HE'S ON THE WALL!
=CHUCKLE= SO HE ONLY PRETENDED TO FALL TO DODGE THE BULLETS, EH?
WELL, HE WON'T BE ABLE TO DODGE NOW.
SAY YOUR PRAYERS, BATMAN!
AAAH!
SFX: POOF
=KOFF= =KOFF=
TEAR GAS!
SPENCE, OVER THERE! IT'S ROBIN!

R-ROBIN? WHERE?!
MY EYES SMART SO BAD, I CAN'T OPEN 'EM!

I'M RIGHT HERE!

SFX: FWISH

WAA!

RATS! LET'S SCRAM FOR NOW!

BATMAN!

ARE YOU HURT?
I'M FINE, CHUM, THANKS TO YOUR TIMELY ARRIVAL.

OTHERWISE, I WOULD'VE BEEN THE "CAPPED CRUSADER."
BUT THE BAD GUYS GOT AWAY...

ANYWAY, NOW WE KNOW FOR SURE THAT THE PROFESSOR IS BEING TARGETED.
LET'S GO BACK TO THE HOSPITAL RIGHT AWAY.

病院
SIGN: HOSPITAL

IT SEEMS THE PROFESSOR KNOWS A SECRET OF THE SPENCE GANG.
SO THEY'RE TRYING TO KILL HIM TO SHUT HIM UP...

BUT WHY WOULDN'T THEY HAVE JUST KILLED HIM BEFORE?

DON'T TALK LIKE THAT!
AH...

BUT I MEAN PROFESSOR CAHN WAS HELD CAPTIVE BY THE SPENCE GANG.

THEY COULD'VE MURDERED HIM ANYTIME THEY LIKED...
I TOLD YOU TO CUT IT OUT!

DON'T TALK ABOUT MY PAPA BEING MURDERED!
ALL RIGHT, ALL RIGHT!
SFX: WHACK WHACK

MY GUESS IS THERE'S A REASON THEY COULDN'T KILL HIM UNTIL NOW.

BUT NOW, THEY DON'T NEED THE PROFESSOR ANYMORE.
NOT ONLY THAT, HE KNOWS A SECRET ABOUT THE SPENCE GANG...

AND THAT'S WHY THEY'RE TRYING TO DO AWAY WITH HIM NOW.
SEE?

SHUT UP!
SFX: BOOT

BUT I WONDER WHAT THAT SECRET IS...

I DON'T KNOW EITHER.

ANYWAY, THE PROFESSOR NEEDS TO RECOVER IN PEACE SO HE CAN TALK TO US AS SOON AS POSSIBLE...

BUT BEFORE THEN, THOSE GOONS...

...MAY TRY AGAIN...
SFX: SWISH

...TO KILL THE PROFESSOR.

WHAT SHOULD WE DO? HOW CAN WE KEEP PAPA SAFE?

DON'T WORRY, HELEN. FROM TONIGHT, ROBIN AND I WILL TAKE SHIFTS TO PROTECT YOUR FATHER.

THAT'S RIGHT. HE'S IN GOOD HANDS WITH US!

SFX: WHAP

I APOLOGIZE FOR HITTING YOU BEFORE, ROBIN...

SMEK

SFX: BLUSH

SFX: WHUMP

ROBIN!
WILL YOU WATCH OVER THE PROFESSOR TONIGHT?

SFX: DAZED

HEY, ROBIN!

SFX: DAZED

BATMAN TO ROBIN! CAN YOU HEAR ME?!

SFX: DAZED

THANKS TO HELEN'S KISS, HE'S ON CLOUD NINE!

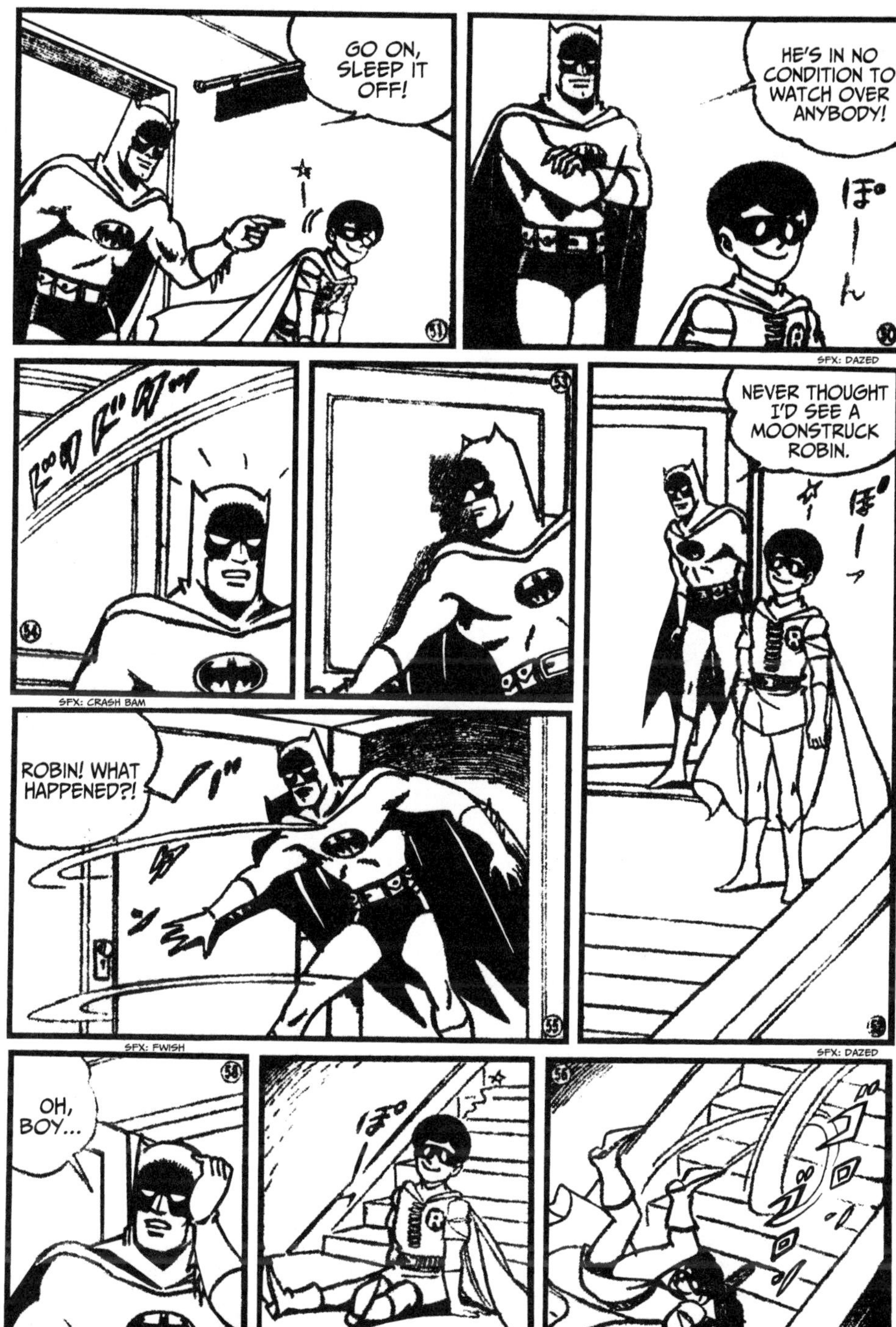
HE'S IN NO CONDITION TO WATCH OVER ANYBODY!
SFX: DAZED
GO ON, SLEEP IT OFF!
NEVER THOUGHT I'D SEE A MOONSTRUCK ROBIN.
SFX: DAZED
SFX: CRASH BAM
ROBIN! WHAT HAPPENED?!
SFX: FWISH
SFX: ROLL ROLL
SFX: DAZED
OH, BOY...

MEANWHILE...
FAILING TO KILL PROFESSOR CAHN HAS REALLY GUMMED UP THE WORKS.

IT'S EVEN HARDER NOW, WHAT WITH BATMAN HANGIN' AROUND...

WHAT THE HECK CAN WE DO?

WE'RE JUST GONNA HAVE TO EXECUTE THE PLAN EARLY.

YEAH, 'CAUSE THE PROF IS HEALING UP EVEN AS WE SIT HERE ON OUR RUMPS!

AND IF HE TELLS ANYONE OUR SECRET...

...OUR PLAN AND EVERYTHING ELSE WILL COME TO NOTHING.

SO WE GOTTA HURRY!

WHEN DO WE DO IT?

TONIGHT!
TONIGHT WE SET OUR PLAN IN MOTION.

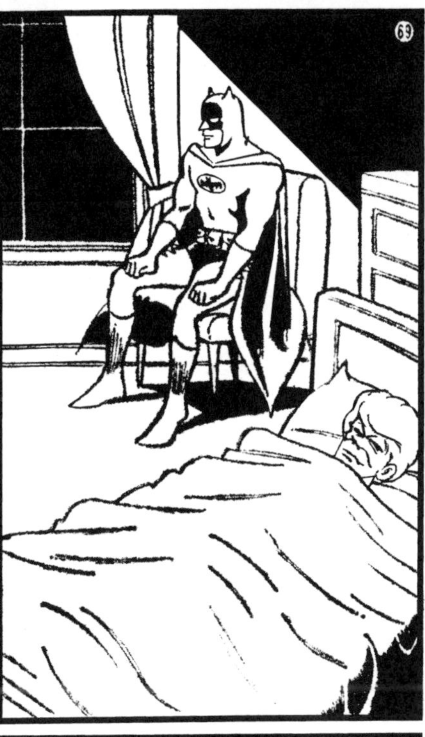

WHAT'S THIS? THE MIDDLE OF THE NIGHT AND PEOPLE ARE WHOOPING IT UP OUTSIDE LIKE IT'S NEW YEAR'S EVE...
SFX: WAAA WAAA

BATMAN! COME QUICK!

ROBIN, WHAT IS IT? DOES IT HAVE TO DO WITH THAT SCREAMING?

THE MONSTER HAS COME ASHORE AGAIN!
IT'S RUNNING WILD IN THE MIDDLE OF TOWN!
WHAT?!

OKAY! ROBIN, TAKE CARE OF THE PROFESSOR!

SFX: ROARRR

WAAA!
WAAA!

IT'LL TRASH THE WHOLE TOWN IF WE JUST STAND AROUND WATCHING IT!
EVERYONE WHO'S GOT A RIFLE, GO GET IT!
YEAH! LET'S DRIVE THE MONSTER AWAY!
THAT'S THE IDEA! RIFLES!

SFX: RATTLE RATTLE

ゴア銀行

SIGN: GORE BANK

WHAT'S ALL THE RUCKUS OUTSIDE?

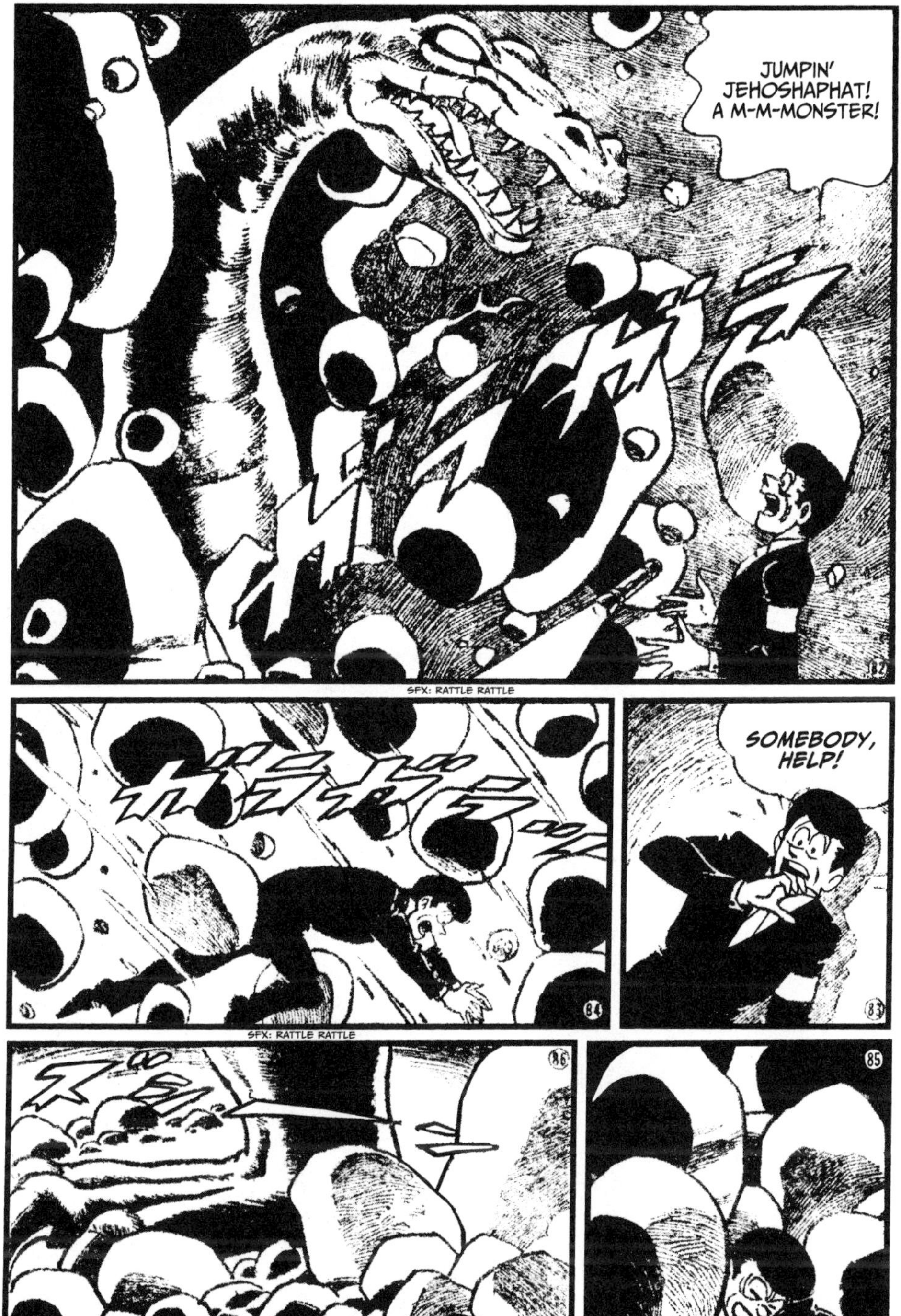

JUMPIN' JEHOSHAPHAT! A M-M-MONSTER!

SFX: RATTLE RATTLE

SOMEBODY, HELP!

SFX: RATTLE RATTLE

SFX: WHUD

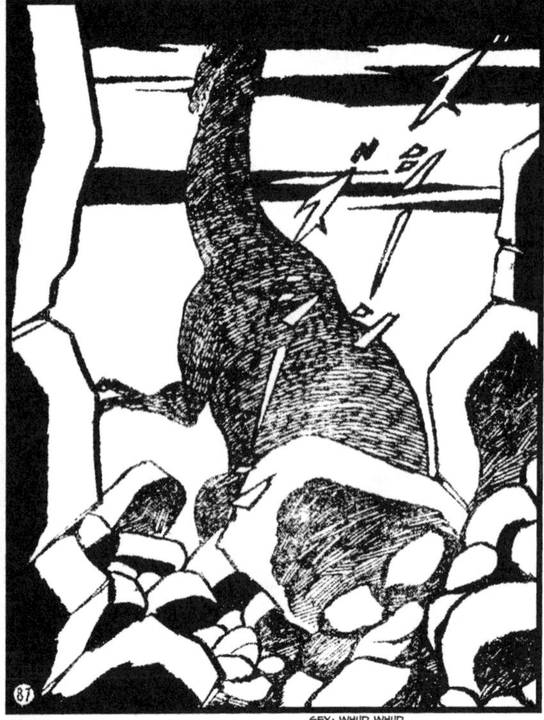

SFX: WHUD WHUD

SFX: WHUP-WHUP-WHUP

BLAST YOU, MONSTER! YOU JUST TURNED THAT BANK INTO RUBBLE!

WELL, I'LL GIVE YOU A TASTE OF MY ANESTHETIC BOMB, WHICH MAKES ANYTHING THAT'S ALIVE FALL ASLEEP INSTANTLY!

SFX: SHOOO

SFX: BOOM

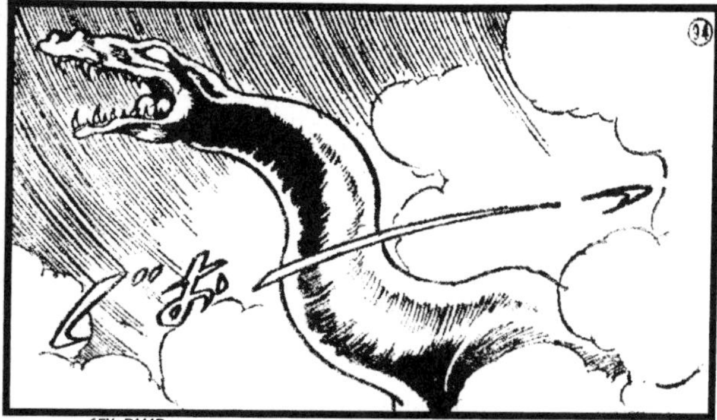
94
SFX: RAAAR

WHA...?! MY ANESTHETIC BOMB HAD NO EFFECT?!
IT DIDN'T EVEN FLINCH!
95

96
SFX: FOOSH

97
AH! IT'S SHOOTING FLAMES FROM ITS MOUTH!

98
SFX: SWISH

99
SFX: BADOOM

SFX: FSSSSSHHH

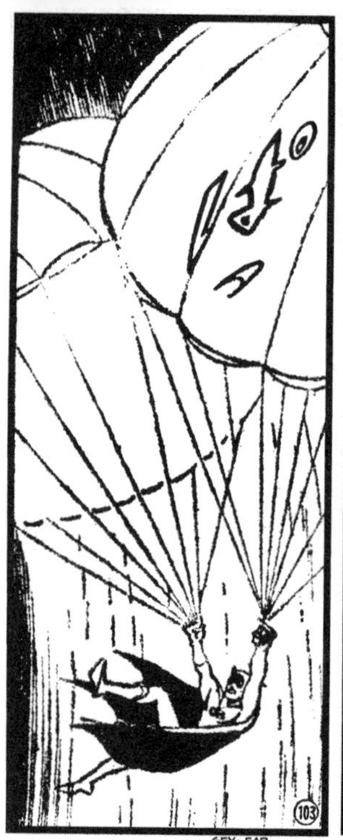

SFX: FAP

OH, NO!
I'M COMING
DOWN RIGHT IN
FRONT OF THE
MONSTER!

バットマン
BATMAN
EXCLUSIVE
JAPANESE VERSION
SHONEN GAHOSHA
©N.P.P. 1967
THE MONSTER OF GORE BAY Part 4
Jiro Kuwata

LAST EPISODE...
When the monster of Gore Bay went on another violent rampage on land, Batman took flight in a helicopter to confront it again. Batman fired a powerful anesthetic explosive at the beast, which retaliated by shooting fire out of its mouth. Luckily, Batman bailed out of his craft right before it exploded, and used a parachute to lightly sail downwards. Unfortunately, his descent was made right before the raging giant monster's eyes...
ROAR
OH, NO! I LANDED RIGHT IN FRONT OF THE MONSTER!
SFX: ROAR
SFX: THUD THUD THUD THUD

SFX: WHUD
SFX: FOOOSH
SFX: FWISH
SFX: WHUMP

SFX: BLAM BLAM BLAM BLAM

JUST KEEP FIRING!
FIRE! FIRE!
SFX: BLAM BLAM

OH! THE TOWNS-PEOPLE!

SFX: BLAM BLAM BLAM

ROARRR!
SFX: BLAM BLAM

SFX: BLAM BLAM BLAM

SFX: THUD THUD THUD THUD

HEY! THE MONSTER IS FLEEING TOWARDS THE SEA!
SFX: THUD THUD THUD

SFX: SPLASH

SFX: BLAM BLAM BLAM

TOP SFX: ZING ZING BOTTOM SFX: FSSSSHHH

SFX: BLOOP BLOOP BLOOP

YEAH! WE CHASED THE MONSTER AWAY!
HURRAY!

WHAT'S TO CHEER ABOUT?
IT COULD COME BACK AT ANY TIME!

THAT'S RIGHT...

YEAH, IT'S NOT LIKE WE KILLED IT.

IT'LL ATTACK US AGAIN, MARK MY WORDS.

...

COME QUICK!

THE NIGHT WATCHMAN AT THE BANK IS DEAD, CRUSHED BY A COLLAPSING WALL!
HUH?

AND THAT'S NOT ALL! THE BANK VAULT WAS ALSO DESTROYED, AND IT'S BEEN EMPTIED! THERE'S NOT ONE DOLLAR LEFT!

WELL, THERE'S NO WAY THE MONSTER MADE OFF WITH IT...
SOMEBODY MUST'VE TAKEN ADVANTAGE OF THE CHAOS HERE AND STOLEN THE MONEY.

AT LAST, DAWN BREAKS...

BUZZ BUZZ, CHATTER CHATTER...
MAN, THE MONSTER REALLY MADE A SHAMBLES OF TOWN.
THAT MAKES TWO VISITS IT'S PAID US.
EVEN THOUGH UP 'TIL NOW, WE ONLY SAW IT IN THE BAY...

THE FIRST TIME, IT LEFT ONE MAN SERIOUSLY INJURED...

...BUT THIS TIME, IT KILLED SOMEONE!

FRIENDS, I SUBMIT THAT AT THIS RATE, NONE OF US WILL HAVE PEACE OF MIND OR BE ABLE TO SLEEP AT NIGHT.

I PROPOSE THAT WE HUNT THE BEAST DOWN!

YEAH! IT'S BETTER THAN WAITING AROUND.

WE KNOW THAT IT'S ALWAYS SOMEWHERE IN GORE BAY.

RIGHT! LET'S SEND DOWN DEPTH CHARGES WHEREVER THE CREATURE IS LIKELY TO BE AND BLOW IT TO HADES!

YEAH! LET'S BLOW THE MONSTER UP!

ALL RIGHT, THEN IT'S SETTLED. LET'S START PREPARING RIGHT NOW, EVERY-ONE!

MEANWHILE...

BATMAN! I'VE BEEN LOOKING ALL OVER FOR YOU!
HI, ROBIN.

APPARENTLY, THE TOWNSPEOPLE ARE GOING TO ENGAGE IN A MONSTER HUNT.

A MONSTER HUNT...
THIS INTRIGUES ME MORE.

LOOK, ROBIN!

YEAH. THE MONSTER'S TRACKS.

SPECIFICALLY, THEY'RE THE TRACKS OF THE MONSTER FLEEING AS IT WAS BEING SHOT BY THE TOWNSPEOPLE'S RIFLES.

HUH? THERE'S SOME BLACK LIQUID SCATTERED AROUND THE FOOTPRINTS...

THE MONSTER'S BLOOD?
LOOK CLOSELY.

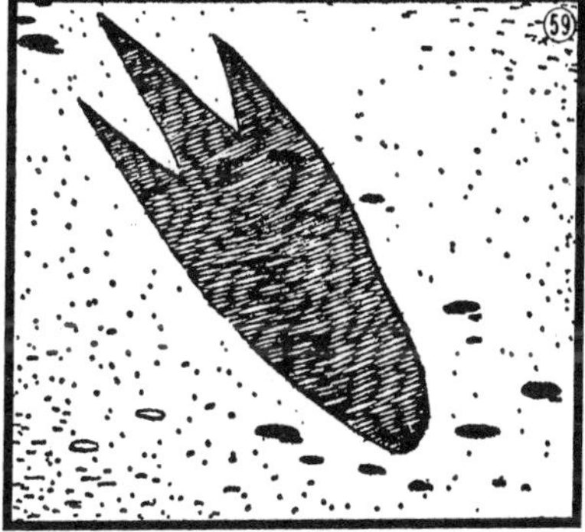

THIS IS OIL!

EXACTLY. THE MONSTER WASN'T BLEEDING.
IT WAS LEAKING MACHINE OIL!

NOW I KNOW WHY IT CAUGHT ON FIRE SO EASILY WHEN I HIT IT WITH A FIREBALL.

AND WHY THE ANESTHETIC BOMB HAD NO EFFECT ON IT...

WHY THEY TRIED TO MURDER PROFESSOR CAHN...
AND THE MONSTER'S TRUE NATURE!

THERE'LL BE SOMETHING INTERESTING TO SEE TONIGHT...

SFX: VRRRRRRRR

SFX: VRRRRRRRR

SFX: VRRRRRRRR

OKAY, STOP HERE.

LET'S DIVE!

SFX: SPLASH

BOSS, ARE YOU OKAY?!

YEAH, YEAH. I'VE BEEN WAITIN' FOR YOU.

WHEN THE TOWNIES ALL FIRED ON YOU AT ONCE WITH THEIR RIFLES, WE WERE WORRIED ABOUT WHETHER YOU'D BE ABLE TO GET OUTTA THERE IN ONE PIECE.

WHO ARE YOU KIDDIN'? I WAS SNUG AS A BUG IN A RUG IN THIS BEAST.

MORE IMPORTANT, HOW ABOUT THIS HAUL, HUH? WE CLEANED THAT BANK VAULT RIGHT OUT!

WITH THIS RECIPE FOR SUCCESS, WE'RE GONNA HIT LOCATION AFTER LOCATION THAT LOOKS LIKE IT'S GOT DOUGH.

AND NOBODY WILL KNOW IT'S US!

YEAH, SINCE THE MONSTER WE FORCED PROFESSOR CAHN TO BUILD IS THE ONE THAT'S WREAKIN' ALL THE HAVOC!

TRUE, BUT WE REALLY GOTTA MOVE ON SHUTTIN' CAHN UP PERMANENTLY BEFORE HE SPILLS EVERYTHING TO BATMAN AND THE COPS!

YEAH. THE IDEA WAS TO CRUSH CAHN DURING THE COMPLETED MONSTER'S FIRST TEST RUN...
...BUT THAT GOT MESSED UP WHEN HE SURVIVED WITH JUST SERIOUS INJURIES.

LET'S SNUFF HIM TONIGHT, ONE WAY OR ANOTHER...

GENTLEMEN, YOUR WORK HERE IS DONE!

BATMAN!

HEY, DON'T FORGET ABOUT ROBIN!

THE DYNAMIC DUO...

DIE!

SFX: BUDDA-BUDDA-BUDDA

SFX: BUDDA-BUDDA-BUDDA

SFX: SPLASH

SFX: BUDDA-BUDDA

RESISTANCE IS IN VAIN! GIVE UP NOW!

OTHERWISE, WE'LL MAKE YOU GO BEDDY-BYE WITH AN ANESTHETIC BOMB!

SFX: BUDDA-BUDDA

AH! BATMAN, THAT'S THE *REAL* MONSTER!

THE GUNFIRE MUST HAVE STARTLED IT AND NOW IT'S HEADING THIS WAY!

バットマン
BATMAN
EXCLUSIVE
JAPANESE VERSION
SHONEN GAHOSHA
© N. P. P. 1967
★ THE MONSTER OF GORE BAY Part 5 ★
Jiro Kuwata

LAST EPISODE...
Batman had a showdown with the Spence gang in the undersea cavern that housed their robotic monster. But then, a genuine giant monster reared its head... the real monster of Gore Bay!

SFX: SPLASH

BATMAN! THAT'S THE REAL MONSTER OF GORE BAY!

YES. THE GUNFIRE MUST HAVE AWAKENED IT.

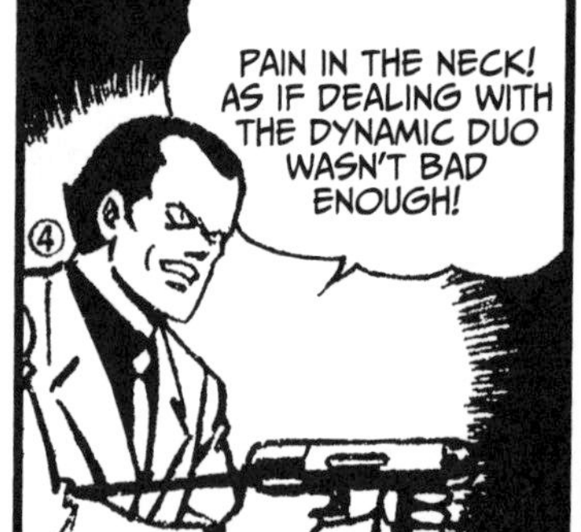
PAIN IN THE NECK! AS IF DEALING WITH THE DYNAMIC DUO WASN'T BAD ENOUGH!

BUT I'LL MOW IT DOWN WITH MY MACHINE GUN!

DON'T DO IT, SPENCE! IF YOU ANGER THAT BEAST, WE'LL ALL BE DONE FOR!

SFX: BUDDA-BUDDA

SFX: CHAK CHAK CHAK

ROARRR!

AAAH!

ROARRR!

HE HIT THE MONSTER'S LEFT EYE!

THAT'S WHAT IT GETS! NOW I'LL GO FOR THE OTHER EYE!

SFX: CHAK CHAK CHAK CHAK

15
SFX: SPLASH

16
SFX: BLOOP BLOOP

OH! THE MONSTER DIVED UNDERWATER!
17

LET IT GO! THAT MONSTER IS ALL BARK AND NO BITE! HUGE BUT GUTLESS!
18

19
SFX: SPLASH

AAAH!
20

IT'S LUNGING OUT OF THE WATER!
21

RARRR!
22

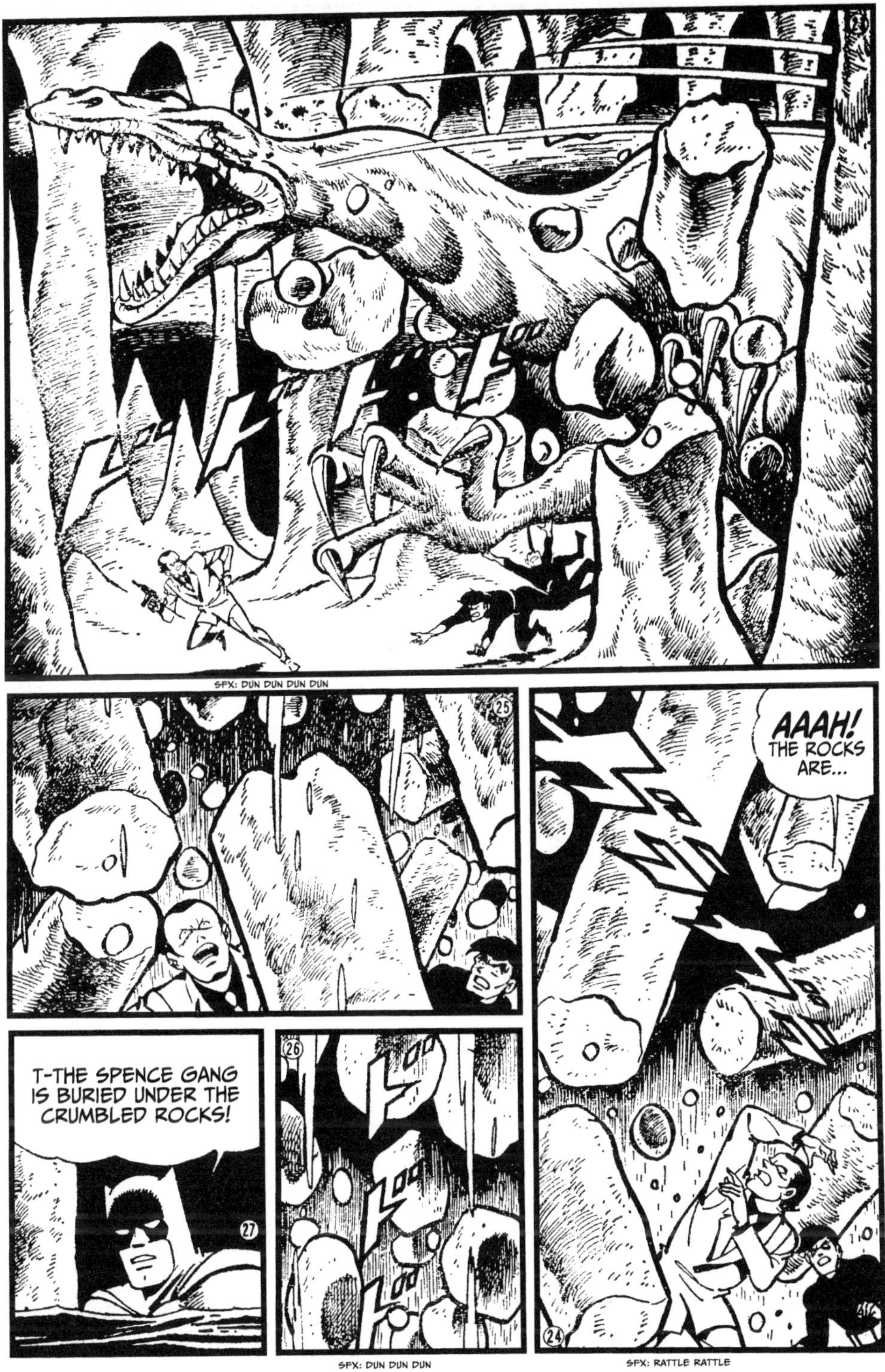

SFX: DUN DUN DUN DUN

AAAH! THE ROCKS ARE...

T-THE SPENCE GANG IS BURIED UNDER THE CRUMBLED ROCKS!

SFX: DUN DUN DUN

SFX: RATTLE RATTLE

AH! WHAT'S THE NOISE?
IT'S THE ISLANDERS! THEY'RE SETTING OFF DEPTH CHARGES IN THE SEA TO DRAW OUT THE MONSTER!
SFX: BOOM BOOM
SFX: BOOM

SFX: SPLOOSH

SFX: SPLASH SPLASH

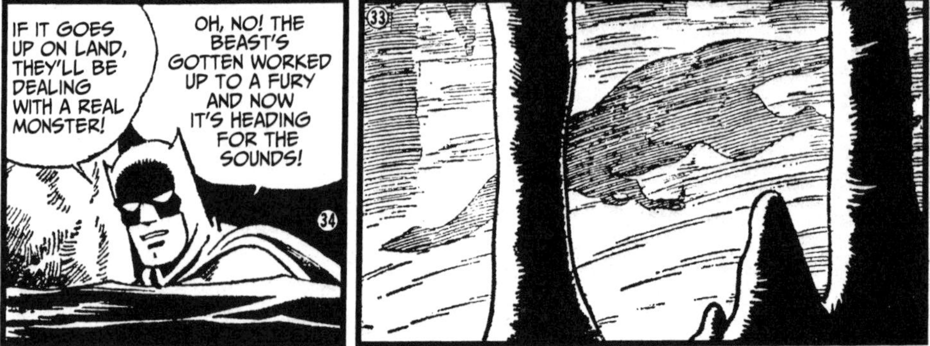
OH, NO! THE BEAST'S GOTTEN WORKED UP TO A FURY AND NOW IT'S HEADING FOR THE SOUNDS!
IF IT GOES UP ON LAND, THEY'LL BE DEALING WITH A REAL MONSTER!

SFX: ZBOOM BOOM BOOM

AAAH! THERE IT IS!

SFX: SPLASH

SFX: BLAM BLAM

RARRR!

SFX: SPLASH

SFX: SPLOOSH

BLUB-
BLUB-
BLUB!

GASP!

W-WHERE'S THE MONSTER?

OH, NO! IT'S SWIMMING TOWARDS SHORE!
IT'LL INVADE THE TOWN AGAIN!

HUH? HEY, LOOK BELOW!
EH?

DID YOU SEE THAT?
YEAH!
ANOTHER MONSTER SWIMMING TOWARDS LAND!

THERE ARE TWO MONSTERS?!

SFX: SPLASH

RARRR!

ROARRR!

SFX: SWISH

LOOK! NOW THE TWO MONSTERS ARE STARTING TO FIGHT BY THE SHORE!
THEY'RE NOT ON THE SAME SIDE?!

SFX: KRAK

SFX: RIP

SFX: ROARRR

WHA...?! THE SECOND ONE IS A ROBOT MONSTER!

BATMAN AND ROBIN ARE INSIDE!

ROBIN, WHEN I GIVE THE WORD, JUMP OUT AND DIVE UNDERWATER!
GOTCHA!

NOW!

SFX: SWISH

SFX: SPLASH

SFX: SWISH

SFX: SPLASH

ROARRR!

SFX: SPLASH

AAAH!

THE ROBOT MONSTER BLEW UP!

SFX: BOOM

ROARRRR!

SFX: SPLASH

BATMAN, THE WOUNDED GENUINE MONSTER IS ESCAPING OUT TO SEA!
I BELIEVE IT'S BEYOND OUR HELP...

I DIDN'T THINK THE EXPLOSIVES THAT WERE PREPARED TO DESTROY THE SPENCE GANG'S ROBOT MONSTER WOULD ALSO PROVE USEFUL IN DEFEATING THE REAL MONSTER.

ROARRRR!

SFX: BLOOP BLOOP

SFX: BLOOP BLOOP

病院
SIGN: HOSPITAL

MMM...

PAPA!

OH! HELEN!

PAPA! PAPA! YOU WOKE UP! OH, THANK GOODNESS!

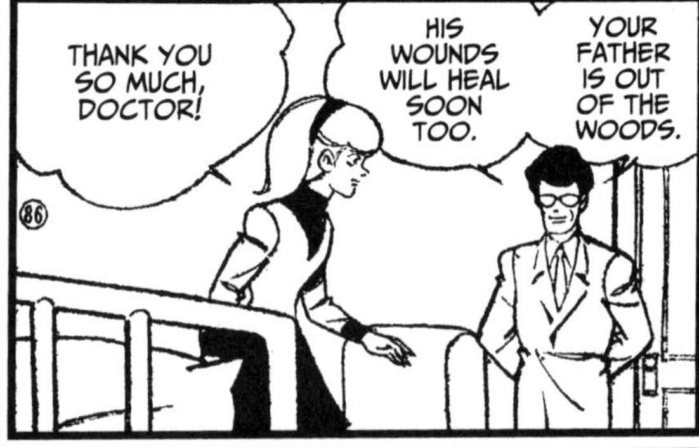
YOUR FATHER IS OUT OF THE WOODS.
HIS WOUNDS WILL HEAL SOON TOO.
THANK YOU SO MUCH, DOCTOR!

YOU OWE THANKS TO TWO MORE PEOPLE.

YES, BATMAN AND ROBIN!
THEY PROTECTED YOU, PAPA.

THEY LEFT YOU A LETTER.
HUH?

OH!

HELEN, NOW THAT PEACE HAS RETURNED TO GORE BAY, STAY THERE WITH YOUR FATHER UNTIL HE'S WELL AGAIN. WE'RE GOING TO HITCH A RIDE HOME IN BRUCE WAYNE'S PLANE. GOODBYE.
-- FROM BATMAN AND ROBIN

PAPA! BATMAN AND ROBIN...
...HAVE ALREADY LEFT.

HUH?

SFX: RRRRR

AH! THAT'S THE PLANE!

SFXRRRRRR

BATMAN AND ROBIN ARE ON THAT PLANE!

SFX: RRRRR

WITH TWO MONSTERS OUT OF THE WAY, PEACE IS RESTORED IN GORE BAY.

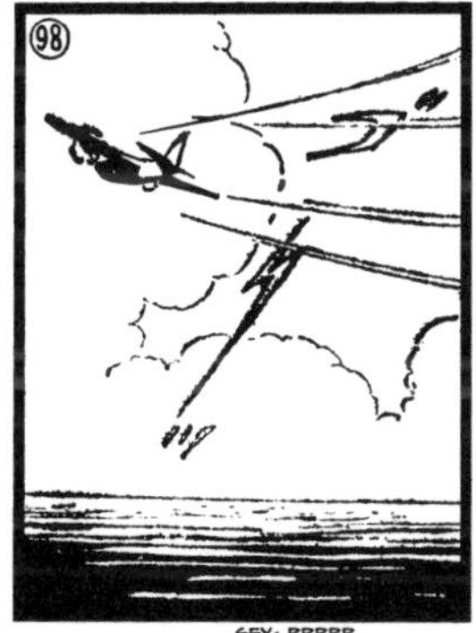

SFX: RRRRR

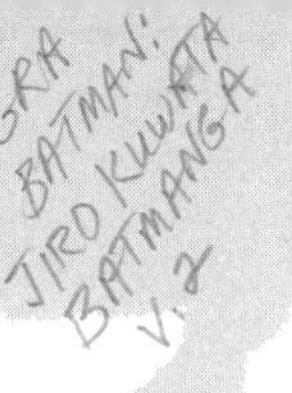
GRA
BATMAN:
JIRO KUWATA
BATMANGA
V. 2

Memories of Batman
by Jiro Kuwata

Batman is one series that holds a lot of memories for me. That being said, I worked on it 50 years ago. Right now, I'm one step away from senility, so most of my memories from that period have faded away.

I do recall that when the magazine *Shonen King* asked me to do a Batman series, my intention was to adapt my art style to the American way of drawing Batman. However, as it happened, I couldn't help but revert to my usual art style, which I regret to some extent. But even trying to stray from my usual form and draw it the American way took me twice as long to do.

At the same time, I was working on multiple stories for other magazines as well, so I didn't have any time to spare. As a result, spending a lot of time changing my style to work on Batman put me well on the way to blowing deadlines for all of the other projects I was working on.

And so, I really had no other choice but to go back to drawing the series with my usual style. But looking back, there's a part of me that thinks drawing it in my own style was the right way to go instead of forcing myself to do it in the American style.

Some 50 years have passed and now Shogakukan Creative is publishing the collected editions of my Batman series for the first time in Japan, for which I'm sincerely grateful. Up to now, many fans have told me they would love to have a collected edition of the series, so I think we're all happy about this good news. My hope is that with this, even more people will read the Batman of my memories.

Jiro Kuwata
October 2013

This essay originally appeared in the Japanese edition of this volume.

BATMAN: THE JIRO KUWATA BATMANGA VOLUME 2

Special thanks to Shonengahosha Co. Ltd. (Japan) and Shogakukan Creative Ltd (Japan)
DC Comics, 4000 Warner Blvd., Burbank, CA 91522
A Warner Bros. Entertainment Company.
Printed by RR Donnelley, Crawfordsville, IN, USA. 6/5/15. First Printing.
ISBN: 978-1-4012-5552-7

Library of Congress Cataloging-in-Publication Data

Kuwata, Jiro, 1935-
Batman : the Jiro Kuwata Batmanga Volume 2 / Jiro Kuwata.
pages cm
ISBN 978-1-4012-5552-7 (paperback)
1. Graphic novels.

PN6728.B36K89 2014
741.5'973—dc23

2014034112

SUSTAINABLE FORESTRY INITIATIVE
Certified Sourcing
www.sfiprogram.org
SFI-01042
APPLIES TO TEXT STOCK ONLY